MIDDLEMARCH

NOTES

including
- *George Eliot's Life and Career*
- *General Synopsis*
- *List of Characters*
- *Chapter Summaries and Commentaries*
- *Analysis of Main Characters*
- *Critical Analysis*
- *Review Questions and Essay Topics*
- *Selected Bibliography*

by
Brian Johnston
Department of English
Northwestern University

Cliffs Notes

INCORPORATED

LINCOLN, NEBRASKA 68501

Editor	Consulting Editor
Gary Carey, M.A. *University of Colorado*	*James L. Roberts, Ph.D.* *Department of English* *University of Nebraska*

Cliffs Notes, Inc.   Lincoln, Nebraska

CONTENTS

GEORGE ELIOT'S LIFE AND CAREER 5

GENERAL SYNOPSIS 8

LIST OF CHARACTERS 12

CHAPTER SUMMARIES AND COMMENTARIES

BOOK ONE

Chapter   1   17
Chapters   2-3 18
Chapters   4-5 20
Chapters   6-8 22
Chapters   9-10 24
Chapters 11-12 27

BOOK TWO

Chapters 13-14 30
Chapter   15   32
Chapters 16-17 33
Chapter   18   35
Chapters 19-21 35
Chapter   22   38

BOOK THREE

Chapters 23-24 39
Chapter   25   40
Chapters 26-27 41
Chapters 28-30 42
Chapter   31   45
Chapters 32-33 46

BOOK FOUR

Chapter   34   47
Chapters 35-36 48
Chapter   37   50
Chapters 38-39 52
Chapters 40-41 53
Chapter   42   55

BOOK FIVE

Chapters 43-44 56
Chapter   45   57

Chapters 46-47 59
Chapter 48 61
Chapters 49-50 62
Chapter 51 64
Chapter 52 65
Chapter 53 66
BOOK SIX
Chapters 54-55 67
Chapters 56-57 69
Chapter 58 71
Chapter 59 72
Chapters 60-61 73
Chapter 62 75
BOOK SEVEN
Chapter 63 76
Chapters 64-65 77
Chapter 66 79
Chapter 67 80
Chapters 68-69 81
Chapter 70 82
Chapter 71 83
BOOK EIGHT
Chapters 72-75 85
Chapters 76-77 88
Chapters 78-79 90
Chapters 80-81 91
Chapters 82-84 93
Chapters 85-86 94
Finale 95
ANALYSIS OF MAIN CHARACTERS 97
CRITICAL ANALYSIS 103
REVIEW QUESTIONS AND ESSAY TOPICS 107
SELECTED BIBLIOGRAPHY 108

George Eliot's Life and Career

Mary Ann Evans, better known under the pseudonym George Eliot, was born on November 22, 1819, at Arbury Farm in Warwickshire, England. She was the third child of Robert Evans and his second wife. The father, a builder and carpenter, managed the estate of Francis Newdigate. Together with her sister Christiana, Mary Ann attended several small boarding schools, and by the time she was about twelve years old, she had already proven her superior intelligence.

When Mary Ann was only sixteen, both she and her sister left school and returned home because of their mother's illness. A year afterward the mother died, the following year her sister married, and young Mary Ann was in full charge of the home. During these years she managed to keep up her studies, which included Greek, Latin, Italian, and German.

As a girl and teen-ager, Mary Ann was deeply religious — owing mainly to the influence of a schoolteacher, Miss Lewis, and a Methodist aunt, Elizabeth Evans. When her brother Isaac married in 1841, Mary Ann and her father moved to Coventry. Through new friends she became acquainted with religious skepticism and freethinking and found it impossible to attend church. In 1842 she moved to her brother at Griff, since their father refused to live with her unless she resumed her religious beliefs and practice. After three weeks she was reconciled with her father, returned home and resumed church attendance, but never again unconditionally accepted the Christian doctrines. She kept her new friends, and under their influence started her first literary work. In 1846 she published anonymously her translation of Strauss's *Leben Jesu (Life of Jesus)*.

When her father died in 1849, Mary Ann inherited a small income for life. Having no longer any immediate duties, the almost thirty-year-old Marian (as she now preferred her name to be spelled) left England, traveled on the Continent, and stayed some months in Switzerland.

In 1850 she returned to Coventry and the same year she contributed her first article to the *Westminster Review*. The following year she became assistant editor of that magazine, a job which brought her in contact with the leading intellectuals of the period. She became a personal friend of the philosopher Herbert Spencer, who introduced her to George Henry Lewes, a journalist and drama critic, philosopher and scientist. Although Lewes' wife had left him, he could not obtain a divorce under the existing laws.

When the friendship between Marian and Lewes developed into a serious relationship, it provoked much adverse criticism. In spite of this, the open relationship lasted from 1854, when the couple went on a trip to Weimar, Germany, until Lewes' death in 1878. The censure gradually slackened, but Marian's brother did not resume contact with her until after Lewes' death. In 1880 she shocked her friends by marrying J. W. Cross, an American banker who was at least twenty years younger than she. Less than a year afterward, in December, 1880, she died of pneumonia. J. W. Cross, who admired her talent and achievements extensively, devoted much of his time to a biographical work on his wife, *Life and Letters of George Eliot*.

Under the influence and encouragement of G. H. Lewes, Marian began her fictional writing. In 1858 three stories, previously published in *Blackwood's Magazine*, were collected and published as *Scenes from Clerical Life* under the pseudonym "George Eliot." These were immediately successful and together with the publication of *Adam Bede* and *The Lifted Veil* the following year, George Eliot's renown was established.

Although she also attempted poetry, she devoted most of her time to a series of novels which were published with intervals of from one to three years. Best known of these are probably *The Mill on the Floss* (1860) and *Silas Marner* (1861), both characterized by vivid, detailed descriptions of English country life and a deep understanding of moral and psychological problems. *Romola*, considered by many to be her least successful novel, was published in 1863; in 1866 came *Felix Holt*, a political novel; in 1868 *The Spanish Gypsy*, a narrative in blank verse; in 1872 *Middlemarch*; in 1876 *Daniel Deronda*, her last novel, which contains two very different plots, one preaching against anti-Semitism and the other showing the author's deep understanding of human psychology and female nature; in 1879 *Impressions of Theophrastus Such*, a collection of satirical essays.

Like many of George Eliot's works, *Middlemarch* was first published in parts. Its history of composition, however, is unique, since it was originally planned as two separate works. It was first intended as the story of a highly gifted doctor, Lydgate, whose career would be interrupted and hampered both by environment and the faults and virtues of his own character. For more than a year George Eliot worked on this story, doing extensive research in medical history, before she thought of combining it with the "Miss Brooke" story which she "began without any serious intention of carrying it out lengthily." It seems, therefore, the more amazing that modern criticism praises the novel for its impressive unity and tight organization. It is today considered George Eliot's most substantial novel, wherein a variety of incidents and characters, and ethical and psychological problems are successfully amalgamated into a unified story of the life of Middlemarch, a provincial town.

General Synopsis

Dorothea Brooke and her younger sister, Celia, live with their uncle at Tipton Grange near the town Middlemarch. At a dinner party at the Grange, Sir James Chettam, a neighboring gentleman, tries to get Dorothea's attention, but she is much more interested in the serious-minded, middle-aged scholar Edward Casoubon. When Sir James offers her the loan of a horse, Dorothea makes him understand that she is interested in him only insofar as he can be a help in her progressive plans for new cottages in the parish. Casoubon, who sees a serious mind and excellent virtues in the idealistic Dorothea, proposes marriage in order to get a companion in his aging years. Dorothea consents because she thinks this will be her chance to develop her mind and intellect.

During a visit to Lowick, Casoubon's home, Dorothea meets Will Ladislaw, Casoubon's cousin. The young man dislikes Dorothea because she is marrying the older cousin, whom he finds very dull and unsympathetic.

Dorothea and Casoubon leave for Rome on a honeymoon which will be combined with Casoubon's studies. In the meantime in Middlemarch, a newly arrived doctor, Tertius Lydgate, poor and ambitious, meets Rosamond Vincy. Although Rosamond is a very egotistical girl, Lydgate can see only her beauty and accomplishments. Rosamond's brother Fred, a charming but irresponsible young man, expects to inherit the fortune of his old uncle, Mr. Featherstone. While waiting for his uncle to die, he gets into a debt which he is unable to pay.

Lydgate is the head of a new hospital, and this brings him into contact with local politics and prejudices. When the Medical Board meets to vote for a chaplain for the hospital, Lydgate votes for Mr. Tyke. Thereby he promotes his own interests, since he secures the good-will of Mr. Bulstrode, a wealthy banker whom Lydgate actually dislikes because of his hypo-critical attitudes.

In Rome Dorothea begins to realize the limitations of her husband's intellect, and she is unhappy. Accidentally Will Ladislaw sees her and goes to visit her and Casoubon. Understanding Dorothea's feelings, Will pities her—a feeling which soon turns into love. He returns to England in order to start a career which will make him independent of Casoubon.

Fred Vincy is unable to pay his debts. He makes a final, desperate attempt to raise money by selling a horse, but the horse turns out to be vicious and brings no money. Caleb Garth, the father of Mary, the girl Fred loves, has signed Fred's note and is responsible for the money that Fred owes. Fred becomes ill, and Lydgate is happy to become his doctor, since it gives him a chance to see more of Rosamond.

When Dorothea and her husband return to England they learn of Celia's marriage to Sir James Chettam. Will sends a note to Dorothea, and this starts a quarrel between Dorothea and Casoubon. The latter falls ill and dies shortly after.

The relatives of Mr. Featherstone, including Fred, are all impatiently waiting for his death. When he finally dies and his will is read, they all get an unpleasant shock. It turns out that he has left practically nothing to his relatives, a great disap-pointment to Fred, who depended on the money. While plans are made for a marriage between Rosamond and Lydgate, Fred is told to prepare himself for the ministry.

Casoubon's will stipulates that Dorothea will have all his property only if she does not marry Will. This gives Dorothea's friends and relatives some concern; they believe that there is something between Dorothea and Will. Mr. Brooks gives up a liberal newspaper he has started and thus cuts off any connection with Will, who was hired as an editor. Will understands that Dorothea's family is trying to separate them, but he refuses to become upset and decides to stay in Middlemarch. When he hears of Casoubon's will, his desire to remain only increases, since he wants to prove that any suspicions about him and Dorothea are wrong.

Lydgate and Rosamond marry, and in order to equip his house according to his wife's extravagant taste, the doctor goes into debt. When he finally has to ask Rosamond to economize, they have a serious quarrel which settles nothing. At the same time Lydgate's practice decreases.

John Raffles, a vulgar drunkard, suddenly appears in Middlemarch. He knows that Will's grandfather became wealthy as a receiver of stolen goods and that Mr. Bulstrode was his clerk at the time. He further knows that Bulstrode's first wife was the widow of Will's grandfather, and when she died, Bulstrode acquired his fortune. Raffles blackmails Bulstrode and the latter is afraid that the true story of his life will come out. To prevent trouble he sends for Will and offers him 500 pounds annually and liberal provisions in his will. Ladislaw refuses, unwilling to taint his honor with the crooked business of his grandfather. Deciding finally to leave Middlemarch, Will goes to London without being sure of Dorothea's feelings for him.

Lydgate goes deeper into debt. Rosamond, who wants to keep up the pretense of wealth, refuses to move to cheaper lodgings. In desperation Lydgate goes to Bulstrode and asks for a loan. The banker, who in the meantime has withdrawn his support of the hospital, only advises him to go to Dorothea for help. When Baffles comes back to Middlemarch in a miserable condition, however, Bulstrode calls Lydgate to attend him. Lydgate gives specific instruction about the treatment of the drunkard. When Lydgate returns next morning, Bulstrode offers him a loan of 1,000 pounds — thinking that in case anything goes wrong, it will be good to have Lydgate on his side.

Bulstrode fails to follow Lydgate's instructions, and Raffles dies. When Lydgate learns of Raffles' death, he is puzzled, but too happy about his money to worry. Raffles has told his story to others, however, and when he dies, rumors start circulating, indicating that Lydgate and Bulstrode have killed the tramp. At a public meeting Bulstrode is totally disgraced, and because he has accepted Bulstrode's money, Lydgate is looked upon as his accomplice.

Dorothea is the only one who refuses to credit Lydgate's involvement in the ugly affair. She resolves to talk to Lydgate, although everyone warns her against it. Lydgate, in the meantime, is in a difficult position. He knows he is innocent, but he cannot openly accuse Bulstrode, not knowing whether the banker actually disobeyed his orders.

Dorothea tries to convince Lydgate that he should remain in Middlemarch and clear his name, but Lydgate doubts that Rosamond would be willing to stand such a period of trial. Dorothea goes to see Rosamond to convince her that she and her husband should remain. When Dorothea arrives at the house, she finds Rosamond and Will Ladislaw together in what seems to be an embrace, and Dorothea quickly leaves the house. Will is furious at Rosamond for having made it seem that he is her lover.

Although thoroughly grieved at having lost Will, whom she loves, Dorothea visits Rosamond the next day to point out why Lydgate must continue as the leader of the hospital, which will be kept up with Dorothea's money. Rosamond feels thoroughly ashamed when confronted with Dorothea's disinterested kindness and explains that there is nothing between her and Will. Dorothea meets Will again, all difficulties are cleared up, and they decide to get married. Although her family first opposes the marriage, Dorothea shows her strength and marries Will. She never accomplishes any of the idealistic goals she had, but she becomes a happy woman.

Bulstrode leaves town with his sickly wife after he has told her the entire truth about his life. Lydgate likewise leaves Middlemarch and becomes a successful physician in high society. Still, he is a disappointed man because he never brings any of his many ideas and plans to fruition. Fred Vincy is given the charge of an estate, and his willingness to work and the income this will bring him, finally makes Mary Garth accept him.

List of Characters

MAIN CHARACTERS

NOTE: Those marked with an asterisk (*) are discussed under Analysis of Main Characters.

*Arthur Brooke
  Country squire and owner of Tipton Grange.

*Dorothea Brooke (Mrs. Casoubon; Mrs. Ladislaw)
  Mr. Brooke's niece.

*Celia Brooke (Lady Chettam)
  Dorothea's younger sister.

*Edward Casoubon
  Scholar and rector of Lowick.

*Sir James Chettam
  Baronet and owner of Freshitt Hall.

Lady Chettam
  Mother of Sir James.

Arthur Chettam
  Baby son of Celia and Sir James.

Mr. Cadwallader
  An unpretentious, good-humored rector.

Mrs. Cadwallader
  A community busybody of shadowy aristocratic claims.

*Tertius Lydgate
  The recently arrived doctor in Middlemarch and director

of the new hospital. (It should be noted that "Mr." is the correct title for addressing a surgeon.)

Mr. Vincy
The mayor of Middlemarch and a textile manufacturer.

Lucy Vincy
The mayor's snobbish wife.

Rosamond Vincy (Mrs. Lydgate)
The Vincy's oldest daughter.

Fred Vincy
Rosamond's oldest brother.

Bob and Louise Vincy
Rosamond's younger brother and sister.

Nicholas Bulstrode
The banker in Middlemarch.

Harriet Bulstrode
The banker's affectionate wife.

Caleb Garth
Land surveyor and manager of estates; a strictly honest and genuinely warm and friendly man.

Susan Garth
Caleb's energetic, temperamental, and good-humored wife.

Mary Garth
The Garths' oldest child.

Christy, Alfred, Jim, Ben, and Letty Garth
Mary's brothers and sister.

Peter Featherstone
Wealthy owner of Stone Court; an old miser who likes to keep his relatives ignorant about his will.

Solomon Featherstone
Peter's brother.

Jonah Featherstone
Peter's brother.

Jane Waule
Peter's rich sister.

Martha Cranch
Peter's poor sister.

Tom Cranch
Martha's son.

Camden Farebrother
Vicar of St. Botolph's and later rector of Lowick.

Mrs. Farebrother
Camden's old mother.

Winifred Farebrother
Camden's middle-aged, unmarried sister.

Henrietta Noble
Camden's warmhearted old aunt.

*Will Ladislaw
Edward Casoubon's second cousin; a young artist and later a good politician.

Adolf Naumann
Will's artist friend in Rome.

John Raffles
A calculating alcoholic who knows of Bulstrode's past.

Joshua Riggs
Peter Featherstone's natural son and Raffles' stepson, who inherits Stone Court.

Captain Lydgate
Tertius Lydgate's aristocratic cousin.

OTHER MIDDLEMARCHERS, TENANTS, FARMERS, SERVANTS

Mr. and Mrs. Abel — Stone Court caretakers.

Mr. Baldwin — tax-gatherer.

Mr. Bambridge — horse-dealer and moneylender.

Mrs. Carter — Tipton Grange cook.

Mr. Chichely — coroner.

Mr. Cooper — farmhand.

Mr. Crabbe — glazier.

Mr. and Mrs. Dagley — tenants of Tipton Grange.

Mr. Dibbetts — druggist.

Mr. Dill — barber.

Mrs. Dollop — *Tankard* landlady.

Mr. Dover — furniture dealer.

Mr. and Mrs. Fitchett — Tipton lodge-keepers.

Mr. Fletcher — Hawley's clerk.

Hiram Ford — waggoner.

Mr. Gambit — doctor.

Mr. and Mrs. Hackbutt — a tanner and his wife.

Mr. Frank Hawley — lawyer; town clerk.

Mr. Hopkins — draper.

Mr. Horrock — veterinarian.

Mr. Jonas — dyer.

Mr. Keck — editor of the *Trumpet*.

Mrs. Keli — Tipton Grange housekeeper.

Mr. and Mrs. Larcher — a carrier and his wife.

Mr. Limp — a shoemaker.

Mr. and Mrs. Mawmsey — a grocer and his wife.

Mr. Minchin — doctor.

Miss Morgan — The Vincys' governess.

Nancy Nash — charwoman.

Mr. and Mrs. Powderell — an ironmonger and his wife.

Pratt — Casoubon's butler.

Pritchard — The Vincys' servingman.

Mrs. Renfrew — colonel's widow.

Mr. Simmons — Featherstone's farm bailiff.

Mr. and Mrs. Sprague — a doctor and his wife.

Mr. Standish — lawyer.

Mrs. Taft — town gossip.

Tantripp — Dorothea's maid.

Edward Thesiger — clergyman.

Mr. Harry Toller — brewer.

Mr. and Mrs. Tom Toller — a doctor and his wife.

Tom — Caleb Garth's young assistant.

Mr. Borthrop Trumbull — Featherstone's second cousin; auctioneer and real estate broker.

Mr. Tucker — Lowick curate.

Mr. Walter Tyke — St. Peter's curate; hospital chaplain.

Mr. Wrench — doctor.

Wright — Tipton Grange groom.

Summaries and Commentaries

BOOK ONE

CHAPTER 1

Summary

   The two sisters, Dorothea and Celia Brooke, both of good family and neither yet twenty years old, live with their uncle, Mr. Brooke, at Tipton Grange near the town of Middlemarch. The elder, Dorothea, is an intense young lady who is interested in improving her intellect and who has several ideas about how to better the conditions of the cottagers in the area. She is the heiress of Mr. Brooke's estate and should normally have been a sought-after prospective wife for any young gentleman of the community. Her ideas about her own capacities and functions, however, are exalted to the degree that they have discouraged men who are looking only for a wife who can take care of domestic chores. Celia, on the other hand, is a more normal girl whose unambitious attitudes and unpremeditated friendliness make her well liked in the community. Mr. Brooke is an easygoing, talkative man who would rather avoid trouble than make his older niece conform to the more general standards regulating women around 1830.

   Early one day when Dorothea returns from an infant school which she has started in the village, Celia asks if they cannot take a look at their mother's jewels and divide them equally between them. Dorothea at first says that she has no use for such vain trinkets, and she asks Celia to keep them all. But trying on an emerald ring, Dorothea realizes the beauty of the gem. Feeling that the ring has a supernatural, religious beauty, she consents to keep it, together with a matching bracelet. Celia is happy that her sister wants to keep them, but when she asks her if she will wear them, Dorothea betrays a shamefaced consciousness of her own weakness. She makes her sister understand that she wants no more questions about jewels and goes back to her architectural plans. Celia silently resists Dorothea's strict attitude, but her good humor prevents her from saying anything openly hostile to her sister.

Commentary

This chapter is a good example of George Eliot's method of characterization. As the narrator, she first explains in basic outline the differences between the two sisters, and then illustrates this difference by means of the discussion on the jewelry. Notice also the slightly overbearing tone which the author gives to Dorothea's expressions of her rather exalted idealism. Already at this point, perhaps, the reader is being encouraged to entertain certain feelings about the main character.

CHAPTERS 2-3

Summary

Sir James Chettam, a good-looking young baronet, and the Reverend Edward Casoubon, an older man respected for profound learning and scholarship, are invited to dinner the same day. At the dinner table the conversation centers on political economy, and Mr. Brooke is the main speaker. Dorothea, who secretly entertains the idea that Sir James will marry her sister, supports Sir James's supposition that the gentry are better off experimenting with new methods to improve their property than just enjoying the pleasant sides of country life. Casoubon keeps silent and when called upon by Mr. Brooke for his opinion on Southey's *Peninsular War*, excuses himself by saying that he has been too engrossed in his own studies to give the book much thought.

This comment immediately catches Dorothea's interest, since it indicates to her that her guest has the same intellectual interests as herself. Casoubon likewise becomes interested in listening to Dorothea, who avoids any silliness when she asks her uncle's permission to put his disorganized books in order.

Sir James attempts to catch Dorothea's attention through a conversation about riding, but Dorothea only gets irritated and wishes that he would turn to Celia, so she can concentrate on listening to Casoubon. After dinner Celia and Dorothea are left alone. Celia points out how ugly Casoubon is, but Dorothea has only noticed his spiritual beauty and intellectual capacity.

When they once more join the men, Dorothea declines Sir James's offer to lend her a horse, pointing out that she is not the kind of woman who desires to be a perfect horsewoman. When Sir James questions her motives, Casoubon breaks into the conversation and points out that motives are sometimes left better unexplained. His attitude as well as language delights Dorothea, and she becomes absorbed in Casoubon's explanations about the Vaudois clergy, while Sir James tries to find out from Celia what her sister likes and dislikes.

The following morning Casoubon is again a guest at Tipton Grange, and Dorothea discovers more qualities in him which Celia is unable to admire. After a visit to the library with Dorothea, Casoubon leaves and Dorothea, on a lonely walk, contemplates the prospect of becoming the scholar's wife. She compares him with philosophers of the past and feels that by marrying him she will be able to scale the intellectual heights she has dreamed of.

She is awakened from this reverie by Sir James bringing her a dog as a present. Dorothea only tells her unlucky suitor that she dislikes pets and Sir James, realizing his mistake, instead discusses her plans for a new set of cottages — a subject he knows interests her. Already seeing in Sir James a useful brother-in-law, Dorothea shows him her plans and Sir James leaves, taking some of the plans with him to see what he can do about making them a reality. Celia witnesses this interview and realizes that both are under misconceptions about each other's interests.

The following week Casoubon is again invited to stay, this time overnight. Dorothea attempts to discuss her plans with him, too, but Casoubon declares that his studies take up all his time.

Dorothea resolves to reach the scholar's intellectual level and begins to visit the library to discover more about his interests. At the same time she chides herself for entertaining the idea that Casoubon might be interested in her.

Commentary

George Eliot often employs the viewpoints and impressions of many individuals in order to give the reader a complex and varied idea of a character. Because the two sisters have different personalities, the sympathies and antipathies of each are more clearly described. The fact that Dorothea likes Casoubon and that Celia intensely dislikes him is actually a comment on all three characters.

In order to understand how unusual Dorothea must appear to her environment, it is necessary to keep in mind the standard Victorian attitude toward women. They were supposed to be accomplished wives and mothers, and as young girls they were trained with this distinct purpose in mind. It is therefore only natural for Sir James to be puzzled when Dorothea does not react to his tokens of interest. Small pets, pleasant rides, and innocent prattle were common aspects of a beginning flirtation, but few men were prepared to court a young woman by means of serious discussions on social reform.

CHAPTERS 4-5

Summary

On a ride home from inspecting the building sites connected with Dorothea's plans, Celia points out to her sister that Sir James must be interested in her as a prospective wife. Dorothea resents this for two reasons. First, she has never been interested in Sir James other than as a means to promote her plans; second, she knows the secret thoughts she has about Casoubon's interest in herself. Celia, whose clear insight is not obstructed by any exalted ideas, explains how unjust Dorothea is in giving Sir James all this attention if she does not include a future marriage in her plans, or "fads" as Celia calls them. That her serious plans are called a fad, and that Sir James is interested in her only as a woman, so disturbs the idealistic Dorothea that she cries from disappointment and vexation.

Dorothea's distress vanishes when she learns, on returning to the Grange, that Casoubon has sent her two pamphlets concerning his studies. While Dorothea is reading these in the library, Mr. Brooke enters and talks of Casoubon as a man who is somewhat remote from reality. Dorothea defends the scholar on the grounds that he is engaged on great work. Mr. Brooke then unenthusiastically tells her that Casoubon has asked for her hand in marriage, carefully pointing out as he relates this, that there is an age difference of more than twenty-seven years. But Dorothea feels both honored and happy and when her uncle persists in pointing out the difficulties she might encounter, she can think only of the happy duties she will enjoy as the companion of so great a man.

Left to herself, Dorothea reads, with great emotion, the letter containing Casoubon's "declaration of love," which she sees as the commencement of an intellectually and idealistically more promising future for herself. She writes her acceptance and, to show her future husband that she will be able to help him in writing his manuscripts, she takes pains to make her handwriting as beautiful as possible. Before she can tell her uncle that she has accepted Casoubon, her happiness is momentarily marred by Celia's comments upon Casoubon's disconcerting table manners. When she learns of Dorothea's engagement, Celia regrets her comment but still feels that her sister has made a disastrous choice. Dorothea's irritation disappears when her scholarly lover comes for dinner.

Commentary

The unpassionately pedantic style of Casoubon's letter and his stilted conversation allows the reader to see that the scholar is not really the superior figure Dorothea imagines him to be. This must also affect our way of seeing Dorothea's character.

We know that her intellectual interests are sincere, but it is also clear that she is the victim of an illusion. This is the beginning of what is often called the "theme of disenchantment" in George Eliot's novels. It is useful for an understanding of the author's concern for human psychology to watch closely the heroine's changing attitude as she discovers the true nature of her husband.

Celia's comments on Casoubon constitute some of the most humorous passages in the novel. Through her reaction to the physically unattractive qualities of the scholar—"two white moles with hairs on them" and "his dimpled hands"—Casoubon and his lofty thoughts are undermined and ridiculed.

CHAPTERS 6-8

Summary

Mrs. Cadwallader, the curate's wife, a woman of aristocratic family, learns of Dorothea's engagement from Celia. She is piqued as well as indignant, for she has already planned a perfectly suitable marriage between Sir James and Dorothea. She goes directly to Sir James to inform him and he naturally is disappointed. A conventional man with conventional aspirations, he cannot understand how a young and beautiful girl like Dorothea can prefer the unyouthful and, to him, totally uninteresting scholar, and Sir James's pride is hurt. Mrs. Cadwallader is aware of his feelings and in order to maintain her position as a planner of suitable marriages, she indicates that the best thing Sir James can do is to start thinking about Celia. Sir James, to relieve his emotions, sets out on a ride and before he returns he has reconciled himself to the fact that it must be Celia if it cannot be her sister.

During the period before the marriage Casoubon spends a great deal of time at the Grange. Dorothea resolves to study Latin, Greek, and Hebrew, the better to help Casoubon with his life's work, *The Key to All Mythologies*. He accepts her offer for its usefulness rather than tenderly appreciating it as a token of love. But Dorothea's motives likewise are mixed. She wants to promote her husband, but she also wants to develop her own intellect. Mr. Brooke declares that such studies are unfitting a young lady, and he makes it clear that engaged girls should prepare themselves for becoming excellent wives and housekeepers — an apprenticeship that Dorothea rejoices to have escaped. Mr. Brooke reconciles himself to his niece's choice of Casoubon with the thought that the scholar might one day gain a deanery and become a bishop.

Sir James accepts the fact that Dorothea has rejected him, and he still visits the Grange. It irritates him, nevertheless, that Casoubon is the reason why he has been slighted, and he feels, moreover, that Mr. Brooke is wrong in giving his consent to so unsuitable a match. To prevent the marriage, Sir James appeals to Mr. Cadwallader, the rector, a man who resembles Mr. Brooke in his reluctance to make definite judgments and who only points out to Sir James that as long as there is no other argument against the marriage than Casoubon's age and physical unattractiveness, there is nothing he can do.

Commentary

Mrs. Cadwallader is one of the many persons George Eliot uses to give her novel humor and local color. She creates a typical busybody who feels entitled to direct everyone's life. Her interferences in people's lives are good-natured rather than malicious, as we see in her conversation with Mr. Brooke. She makes it plain to him that he will appear a fool if he joins the Whig faction of Middlemarch politics and Mr. Brooke plainly feels uncomfortable under the directness of her attacks. By introducing Mr. Cadwallader at this point, the author also draws attention to a world outside Dorothea and Casoubon which will eventually be brought into the novel.

Three principal characters accept the marriage from selfish motives. Casoubon decides to make his declining years more pleasant through Dorothea's company and he suppresses an uneasy intimation that his emotions do not measure up to what literature has taught him about the experience of love. Dorothea sees Casoubon as a means to an intellectually more significant and stimulating life. Mr. Brooke regards the marriage as suitable because if Casoubon becomes a bishop it will bring dignity to the family. Actions motivated by egotistical impulses are one of the author's principal concerns, and in order to see how differently this theme can be treated, it is revealing to watch closely the development of two other characters, Mr. Lydgate and Mr. Bulstrode.

The structure of the novel emerges partly through the account of Dorothea's determination. The core of this plot is naturally the marriage and the numerous people who eventually become affected through it. Dorothea's wish and decision to marry Casoubon involve more and more people, and, to a certain extent, their lives can be seen as effects of one cause—Dorothea's marriage.

When Sir James comes to visit Mr. Cadwallader, the rector is surrounded by his fishing tackle. The description of the physical objects around the rector reveal much of his character and his attitude toward life. Similar means of characterization occur again and again throughout the novel, and they exemplify the nineteenth-century novelists' accuracy in detailed descriptions.

CHAPTERS 9-10

Summary

Dorothea, Celia, and their uncle drive one morning to visit Lowick, Mr. Casoubon's estate. Celia finds the house and its surroundings dull and dreary compared to Sir James's lighter and more colorful Freshitt Hall, but Dorothea likes the dark, severe, and studious atmosphere. Mr. Casoubon asks Dorothea to choose which room she would like to have as her private boudoir, and on Celia's suggestion they all go upstairs to inspect a bow-windowed room. Dorothea refuses to listen to Mr. Brooke's suggestions for alterations and says she wants to keep the room the way Casoubon's mother left it. After the owner has explained two miniatures on the wall, one of his mother and the other of her sister, a woman who made an unfortunate marriage, they all go out into the garden.

Mr. Tucker, a middle-aged curate, serves as their guide around the estate, and he points out that the villagers and the other parishioners are well off and live in good and healthful quarters with tidy and well brought up children. To a certain extent this information disappoints Dorothea, who had hoped for conditions which would require her to continue planning and plotting as she had done in her uncle's parish.

On their way back to the house, they encounter an attractive young man with a sketchbook, whom Casoubon introduces as his second cousin, Will Ladislaw. Dorothea immediately recognizes a similarity in aspect to the miniature on the wall, his grandmother. Mr. Brooke, who explains that he used to puzzle with painting himself (as it seems he has done everyting else at one time or other), makes the reluctant Will show the sketch he has drawn. When Dorothea is asked for her opinion, she points out that she does not understand art; she means it only as an honest admission of her inability to appreciate art, but Will takes it as a derogatory comment on his sketching. This, in addition to her being engaged to Casoubon, makes Will dislike her. When Mr. Brooke questions Casoubon about what Will is planning to do, Casoubon replies that he considers Will an irresponsible young man who lives on his uncle's money rather than having definite plans. Will is invited to visit the Grange, but instead of accepting, he leaves for the Continent six days after he has met his uncle's future wife.

In the few weeks after this departure, Casoubon visits Dorothea regularly, and his work continues to fascinate her. When he suggests that Celia accompany them on their honeymoon to Rome, Dorothea is hurt because it intimates that Casoubon does not include her as closely in his plans as she would like. She mentions nothing of her thoughts, however, and only suggests that it would be unbearably dull for Celia—an answer which is not quite the truth and gives Dorothea a few uneasy moments.

Later the same day there is a large dinner party at the Grange, including everyone of importance in Middlemarch: Mr. Chichely, the coroner and an old bachelor; Mr. Bulstrode, a wealthy banker; Mr. Standish, an old lawyer; Lady Chettam, Sir James's mother; Mrs. Renfrew, a colonel's widow; and others. Among the men as well as the women, the conversation centers on Dorothea and her coming marriage. Some find Dorothea an agreeable, fine girl and believe she will be happy, while others feel that she must be as dull as Casoubon in order to marry him.

In the course of the conversation Dorothea is compared to another Middlemarch woman, Rosamond Vincy, the daughter of the mayor. Mr. Chichely makes it clear that he would much prefer Rosamond, who is lively and not so studious a girl. Among the ladies the talk soon turns to a more intriguing subject, the presence of a newly arrived doctor, Mr. Tertius Lydgate. Mr. Lydgate is a bright, outspoken man with several ideas on medicine. He finds a conversation with Dorothea interesting because he agrees with her liberal ideas, but he also feels that she is too sober-minded for a beautiful young girl.

Commentary

The description of Casoubon's house echoes all the comments previously made about its owner. It is dark, melancholy, colorless, dusty, in "autumnal decline." These characteristics are carried on in further detail to the bow-windowed room, which is pale, with "thin-legged chairs and tables," and it seems a room "where one might fancy the ghost of a tight-laced lady revisiting the scene of her embroidery." As a contrast Celia thinks about Sir James's manor as smiling, blooming, and fresh, and Sir James himself stands with a "handkerchief swiftly metamorphosed from the most delicately-odorous petals." Sensory imagery and descriptive adjectives characterize much of George Eliot's writing, and her subtle humor often comes to light in passages like these.

The main importance of Chapter 10 lies in its function as a transition. The few earlier indications of a world outside Tipton Grange are here fully developed through the introduction of characters who will be of great importance later. After this chapter it is necessary to notice how the author manipulates the major plots she develops—they are all interwoven through transitional chapters like this, and the relationship among the various characters will all be amalgamated into a general, all-inclusive plot which concerns the occupations of an entire town.

By breaking the narrative through author's comments, George Eliot demonstrates another feature of her writing. She advises the reader not to make too hasty judgments about the characters she has so far introduced. Cleverly juxtaposed with this somber warning is her narrative, which describes the social circle of Middlemarch where hasty opinions and prejudices flow freely.

The similarity between the opening and the ending of the chapter also shows its function as a transition. In a very short passage Will, who was of central importance in the previous chapter, leaves England and for the time being the Middlemarch plot. At the end of the chapter, Lydgate, who has been given primary importance, thinks briefly about Dorothea. As a natural continuation of this thought the author slips in a short informative paragraph revealing that Dorothea and Casoubon will leave England as well, but the emphasis is still on Lydgate, who is partly the subject of the following chapter.

CHAPTERS 11-12

Summary

Lydgate, when returning from the dinner party, thinks about Rosamond Vincy, whom he finds attractive and charming, but his musings do not include any dreams about marriage. A beginner in the medical profession, he is without the means to support a wife.

Next morning Rosamond and her mother wait for Fred, the oldest Vincy son, to appear for breakfast. Rosamond is irritated because Fred cannot show up at the regular time, and the mother tries to smooth her temper as much as possible. They discuss how Rosamond must get used to the fact that men will have their own ways, and Rosamond's only answer is that she is tired of Middlemarch men altogether. She has been brought up in an aristocratic girls' school, and she is looking for something better than what the town can offer her.

Fred finally appears and good-humoredly he teases his sister while he orders a huge breakfast. Rosamond feels that if Fred can get up at six o'clock to go hunting, he can also get up in time for a normal breakfast and not make what she sees as extravagant demands. The conversation soon turns to Lydgate, and it pleases Rosamond to find out that he comes from an aristocratic family.

Lydgate is the doctor of Mr. Featherstone, the Vincy children's old uncle. In this connection Rosamond shows a slight touch of jealousy of Mary Garth, a girl from a fairly poor family, who is the old man's nurse and consequently sees Lydgate regularly. Mrs. Vincy points out that what the wealthy Featherstone might now do for Mary could have been Rosamond's lot, but Rosamond rejects the idea of herself as a nurse and companion, since she dislikes the uncle's cough and "ugly relations." Fred becomes a little vexed when Rosamond voices a slight contempt for Mary, but forgets it when the conversation turns to his studies, which are not quite as serious as they should be for a man who originally intended to become a minister.

The next morning Fred and Rosamond ride to visit Featherstone. Mrs. Waule, the old man's sister, is already there, informing him that Fred has used his name in order to get credit for gambling. Featherstone confronts Fred with this accusation and requires that Fred get a formal statement from Mr. Bulstrode, the banker, that it is not true.

In the meantime, Rosamond and Mary discuss Fred, and Mary informs Rosamond that she would not marry Fred even if he should ask her. As long as Mary makes it clear that she is not interested in Lydgate, this makes no difference to Rosamond.

Lydgate arrives, and for the first time Rosamond and the doctor directly confront each other. She sees him as a perfect prospective husband and uses all her natural charms to catch his interest. Whether Lydgate has the money to support the high society life she wants does not even enter her mind. While pleasant thoughts about the future occupy Rosamond's mind on the ride home, Fred worries about the statement he must get from Bulstrode. It bothers his pride that he must do this, but the expectation of inheriting Featherstone's fortune makes him decide to ask his father to take care of the whole unpleasant affair.

Commentary

A further complication of relationship is exposed in these two chapters and through pairing her characters, Lydgate and Rosamond, Fred and Mary, Mrs. Waule and Mr. Featherstone, George Eliot foreshadows many of the events to come. Just as in the relationship between Dorothea and Casoubon, Lydgate and Rosamond have very different motives for their interest in each other. Mary's attitude toward Fred makes a striking contrast to the cunning of Rosamond. Mrs. Waule and Mr. Featherstone are only concerned about money—a factor which clearly will determine much in the lives of the younger people. The irresponsible Fred seriously loves Mary, and the serious Lydgate regards Rosamond as a relaxing interval from his studies. The indications of what might happen are numerous, and the contrasts and similarities among the characters explain one of the author's major means of clarifying their different traits.

Since these chapters end one major part of the novel, it is useful to see what has so far been established. The question of love is clearly outlined, and several couples have been described; selfish motives are apparent; money is indicated to be a necessary factor in life; the influence of the environment on individuals is clear. In order to preceive the structure as well as the major themes of the novel, it is important to keep all these factors in mind when the novel continues.

BOOK TWO

CHAPTERS 13-14

Summary

When Mr. Vincy arrives at Mr. Bulstrode's to talk about Fred's unfortunate position, he finds the banker busy with another visitor, Mr. Lydgate. The latter has come to see Bulstrode about plans for a new hospital where Lydgate will be able to serve as a regular physician and also to observe and study closely some of his theories on the origin and behavior of fevers. In pious language Bulstrode informs Lydgate that he is more concerned with the moral than the physical health of the people in Middlemarch. He then explains that of the two candidates for the position of chaplain at the hospital, Mr. Farebrother and Mr. Tyke, he decidedly favors the latter. Unless Lydgate supports his choice at the upcoming meeting of the Medical Board, Lydgate can expect no support for his work. Lydgate shows himself as an honest and outspoken man and replies that, as far as he sees it, a hospital's function is to heal physical suffering. At this strategic moment when a quarrel easily could have developed, Mr. Vincy walks in, and Lydgate makes this an excuse to leave.

Vincy approaches Bulstrode in an even temper which he has promised himself to keep. Rather than admitting that he has never heard Fred use Featherstone's name, Bulstrode starts lecturing and moralizing. He argues that Vincy has given Fred a too free rein all along. Since money and religious piety do not go well together, he is not certain that he should write a letter which would clear Fred in the old man's eyes. Vincy retorts that if money is a vice, Bulstrode lives an immoral life himself, a comment which offends Bulstrode. The banker, who is married to Vincy's sister, finally intimates that he will write the letter in order to prevent a family quarrel. Thus he can uphold his original argument that Fred does not deserve to be helped, and he makes it seem as if he is the benevolent man who wants to avoid a split in a family relationship.

Early next morning the letter arrives, and Fred can go to Stone Court. The uncle's reaction is somewhat different than expected, however. He dismisses the letter with several ironic comments on the particularly pompous and stilted style which the banker uses. Featherstone really shows his malicious pleasure in making other people seem ridiculous when he points out that Bulstrode's denial makes no difference to his beliefs about Fred. Fred has a difficult time keeping his temper, but he remembers that the old man has promised him some money and he controls his feelings. When he finally gets the money, it is much less than expected, only a hundred pounds.

Once he has the money, Fred leaves his uncle to find Mary Garth. Although Mary's face shows she has been crying, she refuses to complain about Featherstone to Fred. Before he leaves, Fred tries to make Mary promise she will marry him, but she answers that she can never bind her life to a man who has no aims and goals. Fred is momentarily disappointed, but the prospect of his uncle's fortune soon gets him in a better mood. He returns home and gives his mother eighty pounds to keep toward a much larger debt he has incurred and keeps twenty for his own pleasure.

Commentary

Mary is full of sense and gentle sarcasm in her conversation with Fred. She is proud of her own learning as well as of her common sense and points out that unlike Fred she is doing her duty toward herself as well as her family. She chides Fred for insincerity and says that he should find another profession if he cannot be happy as a clergyman. Although she is not as fully developed a character as Dorothea and Rosamond, Mary represents a third and different kind of woman. By comparing her to the other two girls, one can better see the major differences and similarities among the three and thus discover some of the author's attitudes toward various characteristics of women.

Chapter 13 immediately follows the chapter describing Lydgate's dependence on Bulstrode and this indirectly clarifies the relationship between Fred and his uncle. Fred has little of Lydgate's honesty of opinion and he accepts the corruption of his own integrity—a definite contrast to the doctor, who refuses to listen to Bulstrode's exaggerated piety, although the hospital's existence depends on the banker's support. Both chapters express the fact that no man can live entirely according to his own will—one of the novel's major themes—and show how different individuals will react to this particular condition of existence. The single instances should be seen in relation to the larger plot, which concerns several individuals in a restricted community.

In order to be fully aware of the further development of Bulstrode, it is significant to notice his constant emphasis on pious, morally correct behavior. By making his comments and actions sound hypocritical, the author prepares for the later story of the pompous banker's complete dishonesty.

CHAPTER 15

Summary

In retrospect some of the more important aspects of Lydgate's life are described. Lydgate becomes interested in medicine early and he pursues this career in order to develop some of his scientific theories, as well as for the position it might give him in society. Although he comes from an aristocratic family, he belongs to a poor branch of it and needs to work to earn money. As a young man he went to Paris in order to continue his studies. While in Paris he impulsively decided to marry an actress who accidentally killed her husband during a theatrical scene involving a murder. When Lydgate followed her to Lyons and proposed, she admitted that she wanted to murder her husband. To the idealistic Lydgate this was quite a shock. For a while it made him distrust women, and he returned to England.

Commentary

This chapter is introduced by the author's direct comments, and this facilitates the somewhat lengthy explanation of scientific research which precedes the account of Lydgate's life. Although the scientific explanations might seem tedious, they are nevertheless necessary, since they clarify how important Lydgate's theories actually are. This should be remembered when Lydgate's development is hampered through his connection with Bulstrode and Rosamond.

The digression on Lydgate also shows how George Eliot considers the reader's insight into Lydgate's character important before she continues the plot. By showing Lydgate's devotion to medicine and his inability to control his emotions with regard to women, the reader will in turn have certain feelings about him. In addition to this the episodes in Paris foreshadow some of the problems which Lydgate will later face in Middlemarch.

CHAPTERS 16-17

Summary

The Vincys are giving a dinner party. The men discuss the problem of whether Farebrother or Mr. Tyke should become the chaplain of the new hospital. The discussion reveals that there is dissent among the leading men of the town. Lydgate enters the discussion only to point out that he is neutral as long as the future chaplain will leave the medical work to him.

After dinner Lydgate and Rosamond discuss music, and Rosamond suggests that a man like Mr. Lydgate will find Middlemarch dull and provincial. She deliberately underrates herself and her accomplishments, while Lydgate, who appreciates her piano playing and singing, becomes more and more fascinated by her. When asked to join a party of whist players, the doctor declines and for a while watches Mr. Farebrother, who obviously delights in the game.

Shortly afterward Lydgate leaves and he momentarily reflects on Farebrother's interest in gaining money by the game, a trait which does not quite fit his role as a chaplain. Lydgate's thoughts, however, soon turn to more pleasant musings about the charm of Rosamond, but even she is forgotten when he comes home and starts reading a book on medicine.

The next day Lydgate visits Mr. Farebrother in order to find out more about the latter's life and interests. Farebrother, a bachelor, lives with his mother, aunt, and sister. When the doctor arrives, he talks for a while to the mother, who gives her opinion on how to obtain spiritual and physical health. She explains that Mr. Tyke is unsympathetic and unkind to those of his parishioners who attend the more popular sermons of Farebrother. Mr. Lydgate observes the natural partiality of the mother, while Farebrother good-humoredly says that Tyke is correct. The parishioners are rightly his, and he should compel them not to attend anyone else's sermons.

The two men withdraw to the study, where Farebrother shows Lydgate his nature collections. Lydgate is interested from a scientific point of view, but wonders whether a man so ardently interested in another field will be a good minister. Farebrother admits that he has chosen the wrong profession, and he envies Lydgate his ability to devote his life to his career. He realizes that Lydgate has come to test him out, and he points out that Lydgate will be forced to make a choice. Upon Lydgate's question as to why Bulstrode objects to Farebrother, the latter explains that he does not teach Bulstrode's opinions and he also occupies his time with work remote from his clerical duties. He admits, however, that the extra money would be a great help.

Commentary

Notice how the author again intrudes in the narrative. She wants to make sure that the reader knows how differently motivated Rosamond and Lydgate are. This clarification will make later incompatibility between the two seem plausible and it simultaneously makes the reader already anticipate further difficulties.

Together with characters like Mrs. Cadwallader and Mr. Featherstone, Mr. Farebrother's mother is one of the important humorous figures in the novel. Her ideas on what will keep a person healthy are typically simple and unscientific, and they become comical, since they are told with much earnestness to a man who is expert in medicine.

CHAPTER 18

Summary

A few weeks later Lydgate is at home, thinking about whether he should vote for Mr. Farebrother or Mr. Tyke. He personally likes the former, although he feels slightly uncomfortable about his tendency to play for money. On the other hand, he knows that voting for Mr. Tyke will result in Bulstrode's goodwill, and the banker's money is important for the hospital, and the hospital will bring Lydgate financial advantages.

When Lydgate walks into the meeting of the Medical Board, the votes are equally distributed, and Lydgate's vote will determine the outcome. Before he casts his vote, the others have already lined him up on Bulstrode's side. This pressure, and the necessity of keeping Bulstrode as a friend, makes Lydgate give his vote to Mr. Tyke.

Commentary

One of George Eliot's favorite psychological problems is demonstrated in this chapter. Lydgate must choose between moral integrity and opportunistic motives, and he chooses to let his true feelings for Farebrother suffer on account of the benefits Bulstrode can give. That this is a struggle becomes even more evident, because it has already been pointed out that Lydgate does not personally care for the banker.

CHAPTERS 19-21

Summary

The scene shifts to the Vatican in Rome, where a young painter, Adolf Naumann, sees a young woman, puritanically dressed, standing in front of a sensuous painting of Cleopatra.

Naumann, who sees the contrast between the two women as an excellent motif for a painting, runs to fetch a friend, and the friend is Will Ladislaw, Casoubon's cousin. Will immediately recognizes the woman as Dorothea. The painter asks Will to arrange an interview, so arrangements can be made for hiring Dorothea as a model. Will, however, is strangely averse to the idea of approaching Dorothea for this purpose. To get out of this predicament he turns the conversation to the higher value of poetry as compared to art and says that Naumann will never be able to capture the beauty of Dorothea's voice.

Two hours afterward Dorothea is back in her apartment crying. Her tears are due to the first real misunderstanding between herself and Casoubon. When she had asked him whether she could not soon be allowed to help him in writing his book, her husband had become irritated rather than grateful. He explains to her that she does not really understand the stress and labor of a scholar, and her question indicates to him that she is impatient with his progress. Dorothea, in turn, cannot quite conceive that the man whom she has considered intellectually superior is not yet ready to do the work which she has hoped would elevate her own mind.

While Dorothea is still sobbing, Will comes on a visit. He soon realizes that his first judgment of her as a callous and sarcastic woman is wrong. Will and Dorothea are alone, and their conversation turns to Will's prospects for the future. He has given up the thought of becoming a painter; he feels that this art form lacks variety of expression. Dorothea admits that she understands very little about painting, and this honesty, devoid of self-consciousness and coquetry, strikes Will as admirable. Will explains that he knows he could never become a very good painter and thus there is no reason for continuing. This seems an easy and somewhat shockingly irresponsible attitude to Dorothea, who is used to thinking that constant exertion is the only dutiful way to live.

The discussion turns to Casoubon's work and Dorothea describes her husband as a sincere man who devotes his whole life and energy to his project. Will gets slightly upset at her belief in Casoubon and points out how worthless Casoubon's work really is, since he is not using the works of the German philologists. This comment vexes Dorothea, partly because of the attack on her husband, but also because of the episode from the morning. The thought hits her that Will might be right. In order to cover up her confusion she exclaims that she wishes she knew German and thus could help her husband.

At this point Casoubon returns. He is not happy to find Will with his wife and silently feels that she has done something improper in letting Will come in when she was alone. After Will has left, Dorothea asks her husband to forgive her comments from the morning and he accepts, feeling it is natural that she should apologize. Dorothea, although sincere in her wish to be forgiven, senses that she is farther away from her husband than ever because she cannot really perceive why she is the one who should apologize.

Commentary

In order to explain the reason for Dorothea's tears, the author intervenes and gives the information through a flashback method. By doing this, George Eliot again gives the reader more information than the characters themselves possess. The effect of this is naturally that the reader can anticipate further difficulties, while the problems facing Dorothea are unknown to herself.

Once more notice the author's use of imagery in connection with Will and Casoubon.

It is necessary to know George Eliot's own admiration for the German philosophers fully to appreciate Will's comments on Casoubon's studies. Clearly Casoubon's research is not anywhere near as revolutionary as he likes to think.

The discussion between Naumann and Will on poetry versus art and the comments which Will makes on painting when talking to Dorothea indicate another problem which occupied George Eliot. Although these comments could be seen only as additional revelation of the characters, it is also useful to consider them as an isolated discussion of an esthetic problem.

CHAPTER 22

Summary

During dinner the following day, Will shows his most agreeable side, and the conversation centers on Rome and its attributes. Since Dorothea and Casoubon will soon be leaving, Will suggests that before they depart, they visit some of the famous art studios, and he offers himself as a guide.

They accept and he brings them to Naumann's studio without mentioning anything about the painter's first impression of Dorothea. Naumann suggests that Casoubon would be a good model for Thomas Aquinas, and the scholar consents to sit for the character. After a while Naumann also asks if he may make a sketch of Dorothea, and both she and her husband agree, neither realizing that Casoubon has been flattered in order to give this consent. Will is delighted with Dorothea's open and innocent curiosity and unaffected beauty, but he is furious at Naumann for taking advantage of her.

After the couple leaves, Will can finally express to his friend his admiration for Dorothea and his dislike of Casoubon.

Next day Will again visits Dorothea, deliberately choosing a time when Casoubon will not be home. Once more Will brings up the futility of Casoubon's work, and Dorothea gets more upset because she begins to suspect he may be right. When Dorothea says that she feels real life might be uglier than any painting ever made, Will gets vehement in his protests and points out that a woman as beautiful and pleasant as she is should not have such gloomy thoughts. Dorothea, however, does not perceive that everything Will says is colored by his admiration for her and dislike of her husband.

When Casoubon returns, Dorothea tells him that Will has determined to go back to England in order to start a serious career. Casoubon receives the news very coldly and dismisses the subject as fast as he can without being overly rude. Dorothea does not mention Will again.

Commentary

Casoubon's vanity comes clearly to light when he so easily consents to sit for Naumann. He identifies himself with the man he is modeling, and as long as he portrays a man with a serious mind, he does not object to what he otherwise might have found incorrect.

The transitional function of this chapter is obvious. Everyone is going back to England, but their meeting in Rome has created new conflicts which will continue in the plot.

BOOK THREE

CHAPTERS 23-24

Summary

Fred's total debt to Mr. Bambridge, a local horse-dealer and moneylender, is 160 pounds. Since his father became quite upset over having to go to Bulstrode and also because Fred's university debts have been considerable, Fred has asked Caleb Garth, the father of his childhood friend Mary, to sign the bill.

To raise the necessary money Fred first tries to gamble with the 20 pounds he kept from Featherstone's gift. When this fails, he decides to go with Bambridge and Horrock, a veterinarian, to a horse fair close by, feeling confident he will be able to do some trading which will take care of the debt. He trades his horse and 30 pounds for a good hunter, which he hopes he can sell to Lord Medlicote for a considerable profit. Weary, but proud of his own cleverness, he sets out on his way home.

Before Fred can sell the horse, it lames itself, and Fred has to go to the Garths with his remaining 50 pounds and his sad story. When Fred arrives, the active and likable Mrs. Garth tells him that she has managed to save enough money to send one of her sons to school to become an engineer. Feeling really miserable for the first time in his life, Fred confesses that he has only 50 pounds to pay toward his debt, tries to apologize, but fears that they will never forgive him and leaves. Mrs. Garth, who knew nothing of her husband's kindness to Fred, first chides Caleb for his foolishness, but she is not the type to linger over past mistakes and together with her husband she decides that both her own savings and Mary's must be used to pay the debt.

Commentary

The relationship between Mr. and Mrs. Garth and their children is a happy one. Although they live under strained financial conditions, they do not complain, and they always try to make the best of a situation. Caleb, who has tried to make money in various fashions, has never been successful, primarily because he refuses to let anything interfere with his honesty and his pride in his own abilities. The contrast to the selfishness of many of the other characters is obvious and emphasizes the sympathetic attitudes and traits of everyone in the Garth family. Fred's parents, for instance, care nothing about integrity and fine principles; they are against Fred's connection with the Garths because Caleb has not been successful and therefore lives on a lower social level.

There are several instances of humor in these two chapters. The author's comments on the snobbery of the Vincys are bitingly sarcastic; the description of Mrs. Garth trying to be a mother, teacher, and housewife at one and the same time is warmly sympathetic; the comparison of Fred's horse to a bad marriage is a good example of how vivid an incongruous image can be.

CHAPTER 25

Summary

Wanting to tell Mary the sad truth himself, Fred goes to Stone Court. When she hears the story, her thoughts immediately go to her parents and the loss of the money which her mother has diligently saved up for four years, and she refuses to give the irresponsible Fred the pity he wants. But when Fred is on the verge of leaving, her own feelings for him, and his apparent misery, make her ask him to stay. Fred takes this as an opportunity to ask her to love him, saying that only she can keep him out of difficulties. Mary then points out to him that she can never love him unless he proves that he is capable of responsibility and sincerely desires to improve himself. Feeling depressed and ill, Fred leaves.

In the evening Caleb arrives to talk to his daughter and to borrow her savings. He warns her that Fred is a very unstable person and she should not become too attached to him. Mary shows that she is her father's daughter by explaining that she has too much sense and self-esteem to marry a person who is as insecure and dependent as Fred.

Commentary

The old miser, Peter Featherstone, does not care for Caleb because the latter is too complacent to be disturbed by Featherstone's sarcasms or financial temptations. This emphasizes Caleb's honest character and sets him even more apart from the variety of people who let themselves be harassed as they wait for the old man's money—the contrast to Fred is most pronounced.

CHAPTERS 26-27

Summary

Fred becomes ill, but the family doctor, Mr. Wrench, assures the worried mother that there is nothing seriously amiss. The next day Fred gets worse, and when Mr. Lydgate passes by the house, Mrs. Vincy, on Rosamond's suggestion, calls him in. Lydgate diagnoses Fred's illness as typhoid fever and gives strict orders for treatment. This leads to dissatisfaction on the part of Wrench, who feels he has been slighted as the family doctor and insulted as a trustworthy physician. Lydgate becomes the new family doctor.

This news is eventually picked up by the town gossip, and the sympathy is mainly on Wrench's side, since he is an old Middlemarcher. Lydgate feels only irritated because a man whom he considers his inferior in medical knowledge is judged as his equal or superior.

Fred gets slowly better under Lydgate's care, and a happy Mrs. Vincy gives her son all possible care, so he can once more visit the impatient Farebrother, who considers the illness an irritating delay.

During Fred's illness and convalescence, Lydgate and Rosamond see each other every day and both are conscious of an increasing admiration and attraction. Lydgate, however, regards it as a pleasant flirtation, keeping his finances and medical research in mind, while Rosamond already thinks of which house she would like to move into as a married woman.

Commentary

By doing what he feels is his medical duty, Lydgate unawares insults the local pride, and by showing no humility when contradicting Mr. Wrench, he aggravates the town's mistrust of himself as an outsider and stranger. Unconsciously he thus starts a subtle, unpredictable conflict which will influence his life more and more.

Neither Lydgate nor Rosamond can actually be blamed for misunderstanding each other's attentions, since both act according to upbringing and selfish considerations. Lydgate flirts with Rosamond because she is the only available woman; Rosamond, brought up to believe she should marry into high society, takes his flirtation seriously, thinking she has found the man who will suit her. In either case personal motives determine the actions and lay the basis for the misconceptions.

CHAPTERS 28-30

Summary

Mr. and Mrs. Casoubon return to Lowick Manor in mid-January. Dorothea is bothered more than ever by the fact that her marriage has not become the opportunity for achievement which she anticipated, and she is less sure of her husband's excellence. Mr. Brooke and Celia come on a visit, and Dorothea becomes concerned when her uncle remarks that Casoubon looks unnaturally pale. When Mr. Brooke suggests English beef and mutton as a good remedy, and Celia announces that she will be married to Sir James, Dorothea's spirits are restored. She is happy for her sister and also likes to hear that Sir James keeps up his work with her old plans.

One morning some weeks after their return, Dorothea goes to the library to join her husband, who is reading his mail. In a manner which indicates that he is displeased, Casoubon lets her know that Will Ladislaw has sent him a letter, including a note for Dorothea. Dorothea is delighted, but her mood changes when her husband explains that under no circumstances will he welcome a visit from his cousin, indicating that this is exactly what Dorothea *would* like. Dorothea feels that she is being unjustly accused of wanting something which would be against Casoubon's desires, and in anger she leaves the room without reading the letters.

Just as she sits down to work off her frustrations, Casoubon suffers a violent heart attack. Sir James, who in the meantime has arrived to visit Celia, sends for Lydgate, who has become the Chettam family doctor. Celia and Sir James talk about how this incident proves the impropriety of the marriage between the young girl and the aging scholar.

After examining Casoubon a few days after the attack, Lydgate informs Dorothea that her husband might live fifteen years, with care. But to sustain his health, Casoubon must have no disturbing incidents and anxieties, and his work must decrease. At this point Dorothea has forgotten her anger and she is only concerned with the health of her husband. She discovers the fatal letters from Will on her husband's desk. She reads them and realizes that Will's arriving at Lowick must somehow be prevented, and the letters must be put away in order not to disturb Casoubon further. She therefore asks her uncle to write Will of her husband's illness and the impossibility of Will's coming. Mr. Brooke promises to do this, but instead of following Dorothea's request, he invites Will to come and stay at Tipton Grange — neglecting to let his niece know this.

Commentary

Celia's attitude toward her future marriage is an expressive contrast to Dorothea's earlier eagerness. The younger, but more realistic, Celia explains that although she loves Sir James, she also sees a marriage as a definite end to her freedom. Indirectly this is an ironic comment on Dorothea's situation, although Celia does not intend it as such. Dorothea married Casoubon largely because she wanted to develop her mental freedom, and instead she finds herself stifled.

Although Casoubon's behavior toward Dorothea seems cruel and unjust, George Eliot makes it apparent that the aging scholar has difficulties of his own, which should elicit our sympathy. He is a man who wants to achieve great, imaginative work, but who also knows that his own intellectual limitations will make this impossible. Knowing that his ideas have been ridiculed by more able scholars, Casoubon's pride still makes it impossible for him to face this humiliation. In many respects his life has become an endless pretense where there is no outlet for his many frustrations. He likewise knows, just as well as Dorothea, that their marriage is a failure. He married her to obtain a sympathetic listener and companion, and when he finds that Dorothea makes intellectual demands which he cannot fulfill, he stubbornly refuses to admit that once more he is a failure and starts blaming Dorothea for a relationship which both wanted but neither has found satisfactory.

These chapters have an important transitional function and show how both logic and consideration for detail play an important part in George Eliot's writing. The two major plots, the story of Dorothea and the story of Lydgate, are brought together through peripheral characters, aided by a perfectly believable coincidence — Casoubon's heart attack. Mr. Brooke's letter to

Will Ladislaw tightens the Casoubon-Dorothea-Will triangle, and because Mr. Brooke has already been carefully characterized as a scatterbrain who has little conception of the emotions and thoughts of others, his neglecting to inform Dorothea of his decision seems in order. As the novel and the various plots develop, it helps to understand George Eliot's form if one follows closely some of the intricate patterns of interrelationships — they reveal again and again how the author leaves no incident unexplained.

CHAPTER 31

Summary

In a conversation with Mrs. Plymdale, mother of a young man Rosamond has refused, Mrs. Bulstrode, Rosamond's aunt, learns that the town is speculating about a future marriage between Lydgate and Rosamond. Mrs. Bulstrode feels it her responsibility to find out the truth and questions an embarrassed Rosamond, who keeps silent because Lydgate has never openly discussed marriage with her. Mrs. Bulstrode then confronts Lydgate with the gossip and lets him know that he has no right to see Rosamond so often if he has no serious intentions.

Lydgate, who still thinks that the relationship is only an innocent flirtation, decides to avoid Rosamond and prevent gossip which has no basis. After a ten-day absence he once more sees Rosamond. She tries to appear indifferent, but breaks into tears. This takes Lydgate entirely by surprise, and feeling both pity and admiration, he declares his love and leaves the house an engaged man. The same evening Lydgate formally asks for Mr. Vincy's approval, a request which is granted at once.

Commentary

In a conversation with Rosamond, shortly after he has been to Casoubon, Lydgate explains that he would rather treat poor patients because they do not require him to be polite about their personal problems and feelings. Rosamond disagrees and argues that treating the well-off should be an advantage because he will therefore be in the right social circles. This conversation foreshadows much of the trouble which Rosamond and Lydgate will have later.

It was mainly pity which made Lydgate declare his love for Laure, the French actress, and he repeats the same mistake with Rosamond. He regards women as helpless creatures, and not until Rosamond shows her true nature, can he see that women are more than house pets.

CHAPTERS 32-33

Summary

The old and wealthy Peter Featherstone becomes ill and keeps to his bed. This is immediately taken as a sign of his approaching death by a number of relatives who gather at Stone Court in the hope of becoming the recipients of his estate and fortune. The old man himself despises them all and refuses to see any of them. He only tolerates Fred, Mrs. Vincy, and naturally Mary Garth, who serves as his nurse. One morning while Mrs. Vincy gives the patient some medicine, and Fred leisurely watches the procedure, Featherstone's sister, Mrs. Waule, and a brother, Solomon, try to enter the sickroom. Featherstone almost has an angry fit, and threatens them with his stick. Meanwhile, downstairs, Mr. Borthrop Trumbull, a local auctioneer and Featherstone's cousin, together with other young male relatives, flatters Mary Garth; they all think that Mary might receive a substantial amount of money for her services.

Mary, sitting with Featherstone the following night, is disturbed in her reflections on human greed and silliness by Featherstone, who wants her to burn one of two wills which he has made. Mary refuses, first because she wants nothing to do with the old man's finances, and second because she later might be accused of having done this on her own account. Featherstone offers her all the money he keeps in a box in bed — more than 200 pounds — but Mary declines. She also refuses to call Fred unless someone is called with him to witness the burning. Featherstone goes into a rage, while Mary calmly sits down in order to wait out another trying period with her patient. When morning approaches, she goes to the bed and finds that the old man has died. She immediately rings the bell, while she watches a scene she will never forget — Mr. Featherstone, dead, clutching the money he offered her in one hand and the key to the cabinet with the two wills in the other.

Commentary

These chapters again offer good examples of George Eliot's humor. The sarcasm which accompanies the description of each relative, indicates how despicably selfish these human vultures are. Trumbull's manner of speech belongs to a tradition much used in the melodrama at the time. In order to appear significant and learned, he uses a language filled with malapropism. The grotesque behavior of the old man is harshly humorous.

Although not necessary for any of the major plots of the novel, the detailed description of Featherstone's death highlights the themes of greed and selfishness which relate to many of the major characters.

BOOK FOUR

CHAPTER 34

Summary

On a cold May morning Mr. Featherstone is buried according to instructions he had left behind. For the last time he exercises his control over his relatives, who all attend the burial, thinking they have been asked as beneficiaries. Mr. Cadwallader officiates at the ceremony while his wife has joined Dorothea, Celia, and Sir James at a window in Lowick Manor, where they watch the solemn, but splendid, procession in the churchyard.

Just as Mrs. Cadwallader discovers an ugly, "frog-faced" stranger in the group, Celia spots Will Ladislaw among the mourners. She turns to her sister and asks why she has mentioned nothing of his arrival. For Dorothea this is a complete shock, but just as she is about to reply, Mr. Casoubon enters, and she is unable to explain that she is totally ignorant of Will's arrival in Middlemarch. Mr. Brooke interferes and explains that he invited the young man, but the explanation is given in such a way that it seems this was done with Dorothea's full consent. Dorothea realizes how unfavorably this must affect her husband, but with company around she has no means of letting him know she has no part in bringing Ladislaw to England. Mr. Brooke, who has no perception of the problems he has created, goes to fetch Will.

Commentary

This is a dramatically effective chapter, which mainly serves as a transition, bringing together a multitude of characters. By letting the reader observe the funeral from the window at Lowick, the author can keep attention on the outcome of Featherstone's will, as well as develop further suspense in the Dorothea-Casoubon-Will plot. Sir James points to Mr. Lydgate and the Vincys in the procession, Mrs. Cadwallader introduces a new character, and Mr. Brooke indicates that he can use Will's aid in his political plans. As will be seen later, these comments and connections between the different characters are deliberate foreshadowings and suggestions of later incidents. They give the later events a convincing origin, and make the plot a series of cause-effect incidents.

CHAPTERS 35-36

Summary

Immediately after the funeral, Featherstone's relatives gather to hear Mr. Standish, the lawyer, read the will. A surprised Mr. Standish returns from the bedroom with the papers and informs a group filled with jealousies and hopes that there are two wills, and he will read the older and out-dated one first. Aside from insignificant sums to various relatives, this will leaves 10,000 pounds to Fred Vincy, while the estate is left to Joshua Riggs, Mrs. Cadwallader's frog-faced man. The second will, however, revokes practically all the legacies of money, including Fred's. Riggs keeps the estate, but the money will go to the erection of an almshouse for old men.

After learning the content of the will, Mr. Vincy becomes momentarily harder on his children. He requires that Fred go back to the university to finish his studies to become a minister, and he wants Rosamond to give up her marriage plans, since Lydgate is only beginning in his profession, with no prospects for a lucrative living. Vincy also makes it plain that his own finances are such that he cannot advance anything toward the marriage.

While Rosamond resents her father's attitude and thinks of ways to hasten the marriage, Lydgate talks to Mr. Farebrother and explains how much he is looking forward to an orderly marriage, which will enable him to concentrate more fully on his studies instead of having to put up with the tiresome company of the entire Vincy family. When Rosamond a few days later tells him that her father wants to postpone the marriage, Lydgate agrees with her that the sooner they get married the better.

Although the doctor realizes he does not have sufficient means to purchase a house and everything that goes with it, he trusts that Rosamond will bring a dowry with her and goes ahead with purchases he cannot immediately pay for. Rosamond, who dreams of a glorious honeymoon which will take her to the Godwins, Lydgate's aristocratic relations, makes purchases and plans accordingly. Mr. Vincy, who wants to avoid more trouble and tears from his wife and daughter, gives his consent to the marriage, to take place in six weeks, provided Lydgate takes out a life insurance.

Commentary

The conversations among Featherstone's relatives show how greed and envy can become sole reasons for existing, and the author's sarcastic side comments reveal how she detests this kind of egotism. The only sympathetic person in the room is Mary, who is also the only one who could have changed the outcome. She pities Fred, who is entirely crushed, but she does not regret her decision. In an indirect manner, George Eliot moralizes to quite an extent in this chapter. Mary, who never had unrealistically high expectations, can leave the room without feelings of anger, regret, or jealousy. Everyone else must learn that egotistical desires frequently bring disappointment.

The use of dramatic irony increases the suspense in Chapter 36. Neither Lydgate, Rosamond, nor Mr. Vincy really try to discuss the financial aspects of the marriage between Lydgate and Rosamond, and consequently the marriage takes place with false assumptions on all sides. The reader knows that both Lydgate and Rosamond make purchases without actually having the necessary funds, and one can thus anticipate problems which will face the couple.

George Eliot's last sentence in Chapter 36 indicates her own feelings toward her characters. Does she blame Lydgate, Rosamond, or something outside both for the obviously wrong decision they make?

CHAPTER 37

Summary

Mr. Brooke, who has bought a liberal newspaper, the *Pioneer*, hires Will Ladislaw as editor. At a time of much political turmoil, Brooke's decision elicits some criticism both in Middlemarch and among his relatives — they all feel that he should take care of his own tenants before he starts meddling with politics.

Will, in the meantime, comes to admire Dorothea more and more, and his dislike for Casoubon grows proportionately. Determined to see Dorothea, he places himself outside Lowick in a spot where Dorothea must see him, but it starts raining, and taking refuge in the house, Will finds Dorothea alone at home. They discuss Casoubon's work, and Will, who gets irritated when Dorothea praises her husband, blames her for doing dull work for a man with limited ideas. Dorothea has no actual answer to this, since she has discovered more and more of her husband's true character. At the same time she appreciates Will, who can listen to her own ideas and reflections, and it delights her that Will has become her uncle's aide.

When Casoubon returns, Dorothea informs him of Will's visit and his plans for the future. Casoubon becomes visibly irritated and without Dorothea's knowledge he writes Will and explains that if Will accepts Brooke's offer, he will no longer be received at Lowick Manor.

Will has told Dorothea that his grandmother and mother have been treated unjustly by the Casoubon family, and Dorothea suggests to her husband that he make provisions in his will which can make good this injustice. The suspicious Casoubon misconstrues Dorothea's kindness and makes her understand that he wants to hear no more about his cousin. His anger frightens a silenced Dorothea.

The next day Casoubon receives from Will a letter wherein the latter explains that he will remain with Brooke, and Casoubon takes this as more evidence that Will is trying to ruin his marriage.

Commentary

Although this chapter advances the plot, its main purpose is to complete the portrait of Casoubon as a man who is incapable of seeing reality as it is. Because of his own mediocre nature he suspects Will of having dishonest motives, and although he has no evidence, he includes Dorothea in his suspicions. Still, he obviously suffers under his own misconceptions and becomes pitiful rather than contemptible.

CHAPTERS 38-39

Summary

Sir James, desiring support for his feeling that Brooke's political enthusiasm and ownership of the *Pioneer* are wrong, comes to lunch at the Cadwalladers. Just as they all agree about the impropriety of Brooke's actions, Brooke walks in. Sir James shows him a vicious attack, which has appeared in the opposing newspaper, the *Trumpet*, making Brooke seem ludicrous as well as incompetent; it charges that he neglects his own estate and tenants while he writes about political reform.

On Sir James's request Dorothea goes to Tipton Grange to speak to her uncle about the plans she once made for new cottages. When she is shown into the library, Will is there as well, but to his great disappointment Dorothea addresses only her uncle. A servant enters and informs Brooke that the son of Mr. Dagley, one of the cottagers, has killed a young hare, and Brooke leaves the room. Will takes the opportunity to inform Dorothea about Casoubon's letter. She senses how unjustly her husband has acted, but can only silently regret the fact, finding it her duty to be loyal to her husband.

Brooke and Dorothea pay a visit to Freshitt Hall, and on the way they stop at Dagley's cottage. The cottager has just returned from the market and the local tavern. Brooke explains about the boy, and Dagley gets furious at Brooke for complaining about such insignificant things when he should be concerned with the welfare of his tenants, and Brooke barely escapes a physical assault.

Commentary

Before Brooke enters the room, the conversation between the Cadwalladers and Sir James centers on Will, and both Sir

James and Mrs. Cadwallader feel that Will is a suspicious man because he has foreign blood in his veins and has never lived in Middlemarch. This shows how small and provincial Middlemarch actually is. A stranger will be condemned as unwanted simply because he comes from the unknown outside. The author's comments on such limited views and lack of toleration should be kept in mind when the story of Lydgate develops.

The Dagley episode demonstrates George Eliot's sympathetic concern for the deplorable living conditions of the cottagers, and the general dissatisfaction with Brooke's inability to give his tenants decent housing and working facilities is a little piece of direct social criticism. It is interesting to compare this aspect of the novel to parallel situations in Dickens' *Hard Times* and Mrs. Gaskell's *Mary Barton*—novels which are more directly concerned with the social evils of the nineteenth century.

CHAPTERS 40-41

Summary

One morning Caleb Garth surveys his mail while the rest of the family surrounds him. Mary explains that she has been offered a teaching position, and although she would rather stay at home, she informs her parents that she will accept it. Caleb interrupts the chatting and joking by explaining the surprising content of one of his letters. Sir James offers him the position as manager of Freshitt Hall and at the same time mentions that Brooke would like him to resume the management of Tipton Grange, a job which terminated twelve years ago because of a misunderstanding. This is good news to the relatively poor family, and Caleb tells Mary that she can now remain at home.

In the evening Mr. Farebrother comes on a visit. He joins them in their happiness and then tells them the reason for his visit. Fred Vincy has told him how thoroughly ashamed he is, and has asked Farebrother to say good-bye to the Garths for him; he is returning to the university. After the vicar is gone, Caleb suggests to his wife that he might take Fred as an apprentice, knowing that Fred has no desire to become a minister. His wife, who is not quite so tolerant, points out that Fred's snobbish family would never consent, and they would regard such kindness as an attempt to make Fred marry Mary, a thought which does not please Mrs. Garth.

Both Mr. Bulstrode and Joshua Riggs have spoken to Caleb about evaluations of Stone Court, and Caleb wonders if Riggs is planning a sale.

Riggs is visited by Mr. John Raffles, his stepfather—an irresponsible drunkard—who tries to make Riggs give him money by appealing to Riggs's feeling for his mother. Riggs, who remembers how miserable Raffles made his childhood, sends Raffles away after he has given him only a sovereign and some brandy for his flask. Before Raffles leaves, he picks up a paper with Nicholas Bulstrode's signature. Without noticing the name, Raffles crumples the paper and puts it between the flask and its leather covering, which is coming loose.

Commentary

This is the second description of the Garth family and it should be viewed as presenting a happy contrast to the conflicts, misunderstandings, and problems surrounding the other major characters. Evidently their happiness is due to everyone's complete honesty and ability to share good as well as bad things.

Notice how these chapters tighten the different plots. Garth will become involved with Chettam and Brooke, and there is an indication of a future contact between Garth and Bulstrode. Farebrother is a close friend of the Garths and he also has a serious interest in Fred.

By mentioning a second time the paper which Raffles uses to support his bottle, the author impresses on the mind of the reader the existence of the paper. In nineteenth-century melodrama this was a much used device. A single object was given undue emphasis, and as the drama developed, this object became a major element in giving the plot a logical and probable sequence.

CHAPTER 42

Summary

Mr. Casoubon asks Mr. Lydgate to come for a visit because he wants to know the truth about his illness, Lydgate informs him that with care he can live another fifteen to twenty years, but sudden death might occur.

After Lydgate has left, Dorothea joins her husband in the garden. She familiarly puts her arm under his, but Casoubon keeps quiet and aloof, letting her know he would like to be left alone in the library. Dorothea cannot understand this attitude and alone in her room she realizes what a total failure their marriage has been. Instead of pitying her husband, she feels resentment and admits to herself that he is more to blame because he never gives her any reasons for his coldness. In the evening, after her anger has subsided, she waits in the dark for her husband to come out of the library. He is pleased to find her, and together, with her hand in his, they walk "along the broad corridor together."

Commentary

Dorothea's realization of the mediocrity of her husband's mind and his inexplicable behavior toward her are part of the disenchantment which she must go through. Her reaction is resentment, but by never openly showing this feeling to her husband, she proves herself the better, less selfish person of the two.

The "Three Love Problems" treated in Book IV are those of Dorothea and Casoubon; Rosamond and Lydgate; Mary and Fred. In all three relationships personal ambitions and motivations frequently obstruct objective judgments, and George Eliot seems to emphasize over and over the importance of honesty toward others as well as oneself as absolutely necessary.

Notice also the economical transition managed by the last sentence.

BOOK FIVE

CHAPTERS 43-44

Summary

A few days later Casoubon starts rearranging his notes and explains to Dorothea his plans for his book—a confidence he has never given her before. This, in addition to his strange moods, makes Dorothea decide to find out what Mr. Lydgate has told her husband; she is afraid the doctor has given her husband some real reason for making these arrangements. She goes to see Lydgate, but the doctor is out and instead she finds Will with Rosamond. Although happy to meet the doctor's wife and delighted to see Will, Dorothea suddenly decides to go to the hospital to see Lydgate instead of waiting for him. In the carriage she reflects on her sudden decision. She knows she wants to avoid Will in order not to have any secrets from her husband, but she also admits a slight feeling of disappointment in seeing Rosamond alone with Will—a situation which once was hers.

Rosamond asks Will what he thinks of Casoubon's wife, and Will tells her that Dorothea is a woman whose total presence prevents a man from judging details of her physical appearance.

Later Lydgate returns and tells his wife that Dorothea will contribute money to the new hospital, while Rosamond informs her husband that Will is an obvious admirer of Dorothea.

During Dorothea's visit to the hospital, Lydgate explains to her some of his difficulties. Several people in Middlemarch try to stop the progress of the hospital because Bulstrode is its founder and main supporter, and the other doctors are antagonistic because Lydgate was put in charge. Dorothea, who gets indignant at such pettiness, sees the hospital as an opportunity for resuming her charitable work and promises Lydgate 200 pounds a year. When Dorothea explains this to her husband, he makes no objection and asks no questions. He realizes, however, her actual reason for going to see the doctor, and when she mentions nothing of that conversation, his distrust of her increases.

Commentary

The confirmation of Rosamond and Dorothea emphasizes the difference between the two young women. The shallow Rosamond is interested in Dorothea's looks and social position, while the humane Dorothea worries about the quarrel between her husband and Will, and the future of the hospital.

Chapter 44 shows how George Eliot sometimes breaks the sequence of her narrative by describing certain events in retrospect. The previous chapter ends with Lydgate's coming home after his conversation with Dorothea, and in the following chapter we learn what actually took place during the interview. There are two main reasons for this "flashback": the novel describes a multitude of characters, and in order to explain how they become more and more interrelated, the author must give the reader plausible actions and conversations whereby the characters are brought together; a direct account of the episode is dramatically more effective than having Lydgate report to his wife what happened between him and Dorothea.

Since Dorothea and Lydgate are the two major characters of the novel, George Eliot gives them traits and interests in common, which facilitate a plausible connection between the two. Both are seriously occupied with the welfare of mankind in general and both are restricted in their plans by the prejudices of their environments and their marriage partners.

CHAPTER 45

Summary

Instead of accepting Lydgate's medical methods, which are advanced, several people complain about his deviations from the practice of the other Middlemarch doctors. Without realizing the damage he is doing himself, Lydgate informs Mr. Mawmsey, the grocer, that he has no respect for doctors who make a living for themselves by prescribing worthless medicines.

Lydgate means this as a criticism of the backwardness of the medical profession in general, but his words, distorted by local gossipers, reach other Middlemarch doctors as a direct attack on their methods. This, in addition to knowing that Lydgate has been successful in cases which they have given up, makes the doctors regard Lydgate as a nuisance and menace. Lydgate's connection with Bulstrode further damages his reputation. The banker is regarded as a religious hypocrite, and the doctor is adjudged a medical charlatan.

Lydgate mentions the local prejudice against him to Mr. Farebrother, and the latter gives him some advice. He warns the doctor to associate as little as possible with Bulstrode, and to stay out of debt. Lydgate realizes vaguely the truth in Farebrother's comments, but as he points out to Rosamond — being a reformer in his field, he cannot expect his course to be always smooth, and with full confidence in his powers, he disregards most of the criticism.

Commentary

The attitude toward Lydgate shows how society's prejudice and personal bias can become determinative factors in the life of the individual — a favorite theme with George Eliot. Lydgate disregards local opinions because he feels they are results of ignorance and envy. Taking pride in his profession, he makes decisions which he knows are medically correct and cares little about the hurt feelings of the other doctors. What Lydgate has not learned is the diplomacy needed to smooth over the actions he takes; he stubbornly refuses to defer to people he considers professionally or socially inferior. The indication of the "flaw" in Lydgate's character foreshadows much of his later trouble. Mr. Farebrother's remarks serve a similar function; they point directly to events which will happen much later in the novel.

Summary

In addition to gossiping about Lydgate, the Middlemarchers are busy discussing Lord Russell's Reform Bill, currently under debate in the House of Commons. Mr. Brooke favors the bill, primarily as a means of being elected to Parliament; Will Ladislaw is seriously interested in the political situation and uses his rhetorical talents in a series of articles in the *Pioneer*. He is still suspicious in the eyes of the town — he is a stranger who interferes with local affairs. His easy temper has made him a favorite with the children and Mr. Farebrother's aunt, Henrietta Noble, but aside from these, his social circle consists almost solely of the Lydgates.

During one of his frequent visits to the Lydgates, Will and the doctor get into a discussion of whether one might be ethically right in letting an otherwise repulsive or ridiculous person be a direct aid in promoting a beneficial cause. Lydgate, who remembers Farebrother's advice, states in an impatient, almost rude, manner that he feels justified in receiving support for the hospital from Bulstrode, although he does not personally like the banker. Will likewise makes it clear that he works for Brooke because the older man gives him a chance to work with problems which interest him. Trying to defend their own uneasy positions, both become short-tempered, but Lydgate has an additional reason for becoming upset. He has received a letter requesting payment on a bill. In order not to disturb Rosamond, who is pregnant, he feels he must keep the unpleasant matter to himself.

Later the same evening Will reflects on why he actually keeps up his association with Brooke and admits to himself that although he might eventually make a political career he remains in Middlemarch to be near Dorothea. Realizing that he has not seen Dorothea for some time, he decides to go to church at Lowick the next day. Contrary to Casaubon's beliefs, Will has no special desires to see Dorothea an early widow — still, he admires her extensively and feels a certain charm in his own genuine, but distant devotion.

The following morning a happy Will goes singing to church. Dorothea enters and acknowledges his presence with a pale face and a grave bow, and Will realizes he has made a mistake. The thought of annoying Casoubon by his appearance had amused Will, but Dorothea's reaction makes him see he has made a blunder, which might even harm her. When the service is over, Will finally looks at Casoubon, who ignores his cousin, while Dorothea looks at Will with tear-filled eyes.

Commentary

The various reactions to the Reform Bill show the historical and social accuracy of George Eliot's portrait of Middlemarch. The political history never disturbs the development of the plot, and the synthesis of facts and fiction typifies the careful organization of the entire novel. Mr. Brooke, who is interested "not [in] ideas, you know, but a way of putting them," represents the insincerity of those who were on the liberal side only to promote their own interests. Brooke knows the dissatisfaction of his cottagers, but rather than improving their conditions he joins the Liberals to pacify the voices of discontent. The author's treatment of Brooke on this issue is harshly critical and must be interpreted as a comment on current politicians.

The situations of Lydgate and Will are in many ways similar—both find that they must depend on men they dislike or distrust. In their discussion the pride of each comes equally to light, and both justify their connections as necessary means to a great end. This is an ethical problem which faces the characters as well as the reader. Is man actually free to choose his own means, or should society as well as personal integrity impose certain restrictions?

The description of Will indicates that he should be seen in contrast to the class-conscious, snobbish world of Middlemarch. He moves between several social levels and feels free to do what he wants rather than to abide by the strict social laws of Middlemarch. He is seriously criticized for his nonchalant attitude, but also seems to get away with it. Would a Middlemarcher be able to act the same way?

Will admits that he adores Dorothea and he recognizes that Casoubon's refusal to see him might be motivated by jealousy. It amuses him to think that Casoubon is afraid he might later marry Dorothea and thus gain Casoubon's fortune. This kind of irresponsible humor makes him go to church. In church, he becomes aware for the first time that what might seem amusing to him might mean suffering for Dorothea. Like Dorothea, Will must go through a process of disenchantment, and the episode in church gives the kind of insight he needs to make his personality more firm.

CHAPTER 48

Summary

After the service Dorothea is sorry that her husband will not accept what she feels was Will's attempt at a reconciliation. In addition, her husband is in a particularly chilly mood, and she feels depressed and lonely.

In the evening Casoubon asks her to help him outline the further development of his book, and Dorothea reflects on the change which has come over her husband after Lydgate's visit. Earlier he had never included her in his plans and now he relies on her more and more. In the night Dorothea wakes up to see her husband sitting in front of the fire, and she learns that he wants her to continue the marking of his book. Before they return to sleep Casoubon wants Dorothea to promise that she will continue to work on his outlines. Dorothea, who has come to understand how dull and futile his work actually is, cannot unconditionally give a positive answer and asks for time to think it over. For the remainder of the night she reflects on the dreariness of binding herself to such a task.

Next morning she admits that she has a duty toward Casoubon and resolves to give him the answer he wants. She forces herself to go out into the garden to give him her promise, but when she finds him in the summerhouse, he is dead.

Commentary

Dorothea's decision emphasizes her idealism as well as her strong sense of duty. Although she knows it might ruin her own life, she feels bound to obey her husband — it is part of her conception of her duty as a wife. Contrast this with Rosamond's attitude toward Lydgate's more essential work.

By describing in detail Dorothea's agony and her attempts to postpone her decision, the author creates increasing suspense, giving the reader an opportunity to participate in the psychologically and morally difficult choice Dorothea must make. The startling climax of the chapter is a major development of the plot, releasing Dorothea from the theme of problematic marriage and leaving her future "open."

CHAPTERS 49-50

Summary

The day following Casoubon's funeral Sir James informs Mr. Brooke that Will Ladislaw must immediately leave Middlemarch in order to spare Dorothea's feelings and prevent gossip in town. Brooke, who knows how important Will is for the newspaper, refuses to assent to this, making the excuse that even if he should discharge Will, the young man will not leave unless he himself wants to. The reason for Sir James's impatience with Brooke and concern for Dorothea is a codicil to Casoubon's will, which directly insinuates that there has been something between Dorothea and Will, and that they have planned to marry after Casoubon's death.

Dorothea, still weak, suggests to her uncle that she should return home from Freshitt Hall, where she has been convalescing for a week, to see if her husband has left any message about anything he would have liked done. Brooke evades the entire issue and tells her she would be better off staying with her sister for a while. Celia, having had a child, feels a new authority and tells Dorothea the circumstances of the will. Dorothea learns that if she marries Will, she will lose every right to Casoubon's money and estate. She is shocked and feels contempt and disgust for the perverse suspicions her husband must have held.

Returning to Lowick, Dorothea finds no instructions from Casoubon and her first concern is therefore to find a new rector. Brooke suggests Mr. Tyke, "an apostolic man," while Lydgate suggests Mr. Farebrother, in an attempt to make amends for his vote against Farebrother as chaplain of the hospital.

Commentary

The discussion between Sir James and Brooke offers a good example of dramatic suspense. Without explaining why Will must be sent out of England away from Dorothea, the quarrel indicates that there is reason enough. Vague words suggest that it has something to do with Casoubon's will and his jealous suspicions; the step-by-step revelation of all the facts enables the author to focus attention on the selfish arguments of the two men, while simultaneously keeping the reader curious about the reason for the argument.

The codicil to the will moves Dorothea to dislike even the memory of her husband, and thus a future attachment to Will is made more plausible. Dorothea does not even have pity left for Casoubon, and she can think without shame of Will as the injured party, knowing also that Will is entitled to some of Casoubon's money. The feelings of her relatives serve as a striking contrast to her considerate thoughts. They dislike and distrust Will, partly because of his actions in Middlemarch, but mainly because he might be a means for throwing suspicion on Dorothea and the rest of the family, and worse, he might actually marry Dorothea and the money would be lost. In this way the author immediately builds up a new conflict around Dorothea, and it is again connected with her free way of acting—her relatives are afraid she might actually be stubborn enough to marry Will.

64

CHAPTER 51

Summary

Will, who knows nothing about the conditions of the codicil, feels reluctant about approaching Dorothea—it might be interpreted as a poor man's attempts to gain a social position through a wealthy woman, and Will has enough pride to dislike even the thought of such an interpretation. Since Brooke, on Sir James's advice, suddenly shows a disinclination to invite Will as often as he used to, Will sees this as suspicion of his own motives concerning Dorothea. In the meantime he works on the *Pioneer* and prepares Brooke's official election speech.

Brooke, feeling nervous but confident that he will win the nomination for Parliament, has an unaccustomed second glass of sherry before he addresses the public and forgets his speech. The opposition mock him with an effigy of himself, and a voice repeats every word he says. The mob realizes the ridiculous in the situation as well as Brooke's incompetence, and Brooke finds himself forced to retreat under verbal attack and flying eggs. He immediately resigns as a candidate and tells Will that he will give up the newspaper, suggesting that Will go abroad. Will, who knows his potentials as a political writer and thinker, rejects this. He decides to actively go in for political life in London and ultimately gain the position which might enable him one day to approach Dorothea without feelings of humility.

Commentary

Irony surrounds the thoughts and feelings of Will and Dorothea at this point. Both know that they are interested in each other, but neither can approach the other because of pride—Will because he is poor and Dorothea rich; Dorothea because the codicil suggests a love which Will has never expressed to her.

Mainly humorous, the political meeting is another example of George Eliot's knowledge of all facets of an English town. It paints a true picture of the raucous, often directly dangerous conditions characterizing English political life at the time of the Reform Bill. It also completes the picture of Brooke as a man of many, but only insignificant, words and plans.

CHAPTER 52

Summary

Dorothea chooses Mr. Farebrother as the new rector, and his whole family rejoices with him. Winifred, his sister, suggests that now he should marry and mentions Mary Garth as a sensible, likable girl. Farebrother makes the suggestion seem ridiculous, pointing to his age and set bachelor manners.

Shortly after Farebrother's appointment, Fred Vincy comes to ask his advice. Fred has finally obtained his degree, but he still has a serious problem. Mary Garth has earlier refused to marry him if he enters the Church, and Fred considers this decisive in his choice of career. He asks Farebrother to find out if Mary maintains her position, and if she still has feelings for him.

Farebrother puts aside any emotions he might have himself and goes to see Mary. She tells him that Fred as a clergyman would seem a "mere caricature" to her and she could never respect or marry him. Farebrother then asks if she loves Fred sincerely enough not to consider anyone else, and it occurs to Mary that Farebrother himself might be partial toward her. Although she admires him greatly, she tells him she really loves Fred, and a disappointed, but sensibly controlled, Farebrother leaves.

Commentary

The subtle, gradual revelation of Farebrother's feelings gives this chapter an inner tension. Moving from a general indication of the preference of Farebrother's family to his specific feelings for Mary, the chapter proves that love can be a lonely conflict, but the vicar's favor to Fred shows that it can also be unselfish. Farebrother's lack of egotism is echoed in the relationship between Fred and Mary. Both are honest about their love, and they are both motivated by serious considerations for the other person.

CHAPTER 53

Summary

Mr. Bulstrode buys Stone Court, and one evening the banker happily surveys his new property while talking to Caleb Garth about improvements he wants to make. A shabby-looking man, dressed in dark clothes, comes up the road. When he discovers Bulstrode on horseback, he greets the banker familiarly by the name Nick. Bulstrode, after a struggle with himself, decides to return the greeting of the stranger, who is Mr. John Raffles. Caleb, who has no curiosity, leaves the odd pair.

Raffles talks in a disrespectful tone, while Bulstrode, acting like a man under pressure, invites the tramp into the house. Raffles keeps referring to their previous acquaintance in London when Bulstrode married "the old widow" and paid for Raffles' trip to America in order to keep secret that he had discovered "her daughter and her grandchild." Bulstrode strives to appear indifferent, but offers Raffles an annuity to stay away. Raffles refuses and says he wants 200 pounds immediately and his freedom to go where he wants. Raffles stays overnight at Stone Court; Bulstrode gives him the money the next morning and Raffles promises to leave, but not until he has once more mentioned the woman and her child. Bulstrode immediately returns home, too late to hear Raffles mention the name Ladislaw as the woman's married name.

Commentary

Raffles' hold on Bulstrode strongly indicates that the banker has a past he would like to keep quiet, thus a new conflict is foreshadowed. It is typical of George Eliot's writing that she does not give all the facts immediately. The reader is kept in suspense about any details. In some ways this could be compared to plot-building devices used in detective stories; there are many indications and clues, but only as the regular plot progresses in time, are the facts of the characters' past fully revealed.

The last three chapters in Book V concern three different plots. A previous, gradual convergence of these plots and the characters involved makes it possible for the author at this point to move freely from one to the other without any transitional problems. The reader has been prepared all along even for details; for instance, the piece of paper that Raffles picked up shows why he would come back to Middlemarch. In order to understand more fully the very complicated scheme behind the unity of this novel, one should constantly be aware of how every episode is explained, and how the different plots merge more and more.

BOOK SIX

CHAPTERS 54-55

Summary

Dorothea finally gets tired of staying with Sir James, Celia, and the "best" baby in the world, and on a beautiful June morning she returns to Lowick. Dorothea's family and friends are against her decision, but Dorothea, who thinks this will give her a better opportunity to see Will, defies their advice. Aside from getting a glimpse of Will in church, she neither sees him nor hears of him. She attributes this to Will's knowledge of the codicil.

Finally one morning Will is formally announced. He tells her of his plans about establishing himself in politics in London. Dorothea, who thinks he is doing this because he did not inherit any of Casoubon's money, feels very awkward. Surmising that Will knows of the codicil, she cannot tell him that if it were up to her, he could have all the money. Will interprets Dorothea's silence as an agreement with his plans and an indication of her unwillingness to marry a poor man. Although both sense an emotional rapport, neither can admit this, being unsure of the other's feelings. Sir James enters and breaks the tension. Will leaves, while Dorothea indirectly lets Sir James know that she wants no criticism of her having received Will.

Dorothea goes on another visit to Freshitt Hall. Celia, who is tired of seeing her sister in mourning clothes, takes off Dorothea's widow's cap. This starts a conversation about second marriages. Sir James's mother is quite shocked that anyone would think of such a thing before the year's mourning is out. Mrs. Cadwallader feels it would be for the better, provided that the widow, who has already had one bad marriage, would listen to friendly advice and take the man her friends select for her (Mrs. Cadwallader has already planned a marriage between Dorothea and a lord).

Sir James, out of delicacy for Dorothea's feelings, puts a stop to the conversation. Dorothea, who clearly knows the meaning behind Mrs. Cadwallader's words, makes them understand that she has no intention of looking around for a second, suitable husband. She intends to return to her plans for cottages and explains to Celia that she wants to consult with Caleb Garth.

Commentary

Although Dorothea yearns to see Will, she does not fully recognize her feelings as love. Even when Will leaves, and she is puzzled by her strong emotions and sorrow, she thinks her reaction is due to the breaking of a warm friendship. An awakening to true love is one of the last learning processes that Dorothea must go through, and in order to keep the reader's suspense and to elaborate further on the psychological changes in Dorothea, the author makes this a gradual development.

Will's decision to leave terminates for a while the conflicts surrounding him and Dorothea, and makes it easier for the author to return to some of the other plot developments.

Mrs. Cadwallader's comments that Dorothea should concentrate on finding a second and more suitable husband, demonstrate how restricted a woman's movements and tasks were in the mid-nineteenth century. Dorothea's decision to continue her architectural plans is regarded as unorthodox and eccentric. Instead of admiring her purposes, her friends and relatives feel slightly ashamed of having such an oddity in their midst. Celia's pride and delight in her baby constituted the norm, and Dorothea's attitude toward mother and child shows how she seeks beyond domestic routine for fulfillment.

CHAPTERS 56-57

Summary

The railroad has come to Middlemarch, and many regard it with suspicion and fright. Caleb Garth, now also employed by Dorothea, has as one of his duties to evaluate the property where the railway is being built. Going to survey the progress of the construction, he one day spots local cottagers attacking the railroad workers, and both he and his assistant, Tom, run to the workers' rescue. At this point Fred Vincy appears on horseback, comprehends the situation, and drives off the attackers. The injured Tom is sent home on Fred's horse, while Caleb goes to set right the cottagers, who have acted more out of ignorance than malice.

When Caleb returns, Fred tells him about Mary's decision not to marry him if he enters the Church and asks if Caleb will take him as his assistant and give Fred a chance to learn his trade. Caleb, who likes Fred, promises nothing, but late that evening he tells his wife he will take Fred as his helper and make a man out of him. Mrs. Garth, who has hoped that Mary would marry Mr. Farebrother, is not happy, but she understands that her daughter feels strongly for Fred and gives her consent.

Fred's own family becomes more upset about his plans. Mr. Vincy, who had hoped to see his son on a higher social level than himself, feels he has wasted vast expenses on a son who is stepping down in the world. Mrs. Vincy is highly disappointed because she can foresee that her son will now become even closer connected with a family she considers lowbred. When she complains to her husband about her trials, Vincy only gets the more irritated. He knows that Lydgate is getting deeper into debt and anticipates a complaining Rosamond will bring him more trouble one day.

Fred stops in to see Mrs. Garth to assure her of his serious intentions and finds the whole family gathered around Christy, the eldest son, who has returned from school. Mrs. Garth proudly tells Fred how well Christy is doing, and Fred detects the indirect criticism of himself. She also cannot resist telling him about Mr. Farebrother's feelings for Mary and she blames Fred for being a conceited, impulsive young man, too blind to realize the difficult task he gave Farebrother when asking him to speak to Mary.

A jealous Fred goes to see Mary, who is helping the Farebrothers get settled at the Lowick parsonage. Once he is alone with her, he reveals his suspicions. The thought that Farebrother sincerely loves her astonishes Mary, but with her regular mixture of sarcasm and sincerity, she gives Fred a kind of assurance that he is wrong in his assumptions. Fred leaves in a happier mood than when he arrived, while Mary reflects on the news he brought with him.

Commentary

The attitude of the cottagers and some of the landowners toward the railroad is part of the sociological and historical aspect of the novel. Ignorance and selfish motives often created difficulties for industrial progress. By describing these actions, George Eliot continues her consideration for the general picture of life in Middlemarch and gives the specific events a complete background. In addition, it enables her to use some of the delightful dialects which typify many of her minor characters.

It is characteristic of George Eliot's cause-effect writing that it utilizes the incident between the workers and farmers to develop the plot. It facilitates a meeting between Fred and Caleb, and Tom's injury makes possible a continued connection between the two. Although the incident itself is accidental, it appears natural and consequential because the author has described in detail some of the general ignorance leading up to the fight.

The feelings of Mrs. Garth and Mrs. Vincy are in many ways similar. Both have a certain pride, and they desire to protect their families from derogatory talk. Mrs. Vincy's pride is nevertheless unsympathetic, while we can appreciate Mrs. Garth's feelings. The former is a social snob; the latter wants to avoid being labeled a social climber.

Christy is used mainly as a contrast to Fred; he is serious, energetic, and has definite goals he works toward. His presence aggravates Mrs. Garth's contempt for the unstable Fred and contributes to her feeling that Mr. Farebrother would be a more desirable son-in-law. Christy also influences Fred's view of himself. Fred can see what hard work will accomplish and he learns a little more about how irresponsible he has actually been.

CHAPTER 58

Summary

Captain Lydgate, the doctor's cousin, visits with Rosamond and her husband. Rosamond enjoys the company of a real baronet's son and delights in his attentions. Lydgate, on the other hand, has only contempt for his cousin's stupidity and shallow interests. Against Lydgate's express wishes, Rosamond goes riding with the captain and as a result she loses her baby. After Rosamond has recovered, she tells her husband about disobeying him. Lydgate is angry as well as disappointed, but Rosamond cannot see how she possibly could have refused the captain's invitation *only* because her husband disapproved.

Lydgate's financial position has become gradually worse, and he is forced to make arrangements which will enable him to pay some of his most pressing bills. He decides to have some of their silver returned and wants to use the furniture as a security for a debt. When Rosamond hears this, she resents his actions and regards them as a cruelty toward herself. Her only suggestion is that they either ask her father for money or depart from Middlemarch, leaving it up to Lydgate's relatives to find him a more lucrative position. Lydgate, at first furious, and then frustrated and disappointed, realizes more and more that his wife will become an obstacle rather than a support and aid in his plans for the future.

Commentary

Lydgate's marriage difficulties are in many ways similar to Dorothea's. He gradually discovers the real girl behind the ideal he married, and it is a painful, frustrating process of awakening. Rosamond will never change, and if he is to keep any of his love for her at all, he must make all the adjustments. To a certain extent Lydgate's experiences are more tragic than Dorothea's because his work, of more importance, will always be hampered by Rosamond's mind, which is even more mediocre than Casoubon's.

CHAPTER 59

Summary

The codicil to Casoubon's will does not remain a family secret for long. Fred hears of it through the Farebrother's servant, who in turn has it from Dorothea's maid. Fred mentions it to Rosamond, since he knows that Will frequently visits her. Rosamond, once more acting against her husband's desires, tells a shocked and disbelieving Will about Casoubon's last wishes. Will, who is in a daze, tells Rosamond that now he is forever prevented from marrying Dorothea. Instead of pitying him, Rosamond gets a little irritated that he even should have entertained that idea; she has come to regard Will's attention as a permanent distraction from all the annoying problems her husband presents her with. She already knows that the prospects for the future are rather dark because her father has refused her appeal for financial help.

Commentary

The way the news of the codicil reaches Will shows how intricate the relationships between different people have become. In addition it is also another example of how every detail of the story has its logical explanation and careful preparation. The connection between Dorothea and the Farebrothers, the connection between the Farebrothers and Fred, the connection between

Fred and Rosamond, and the connection between Rosamond and Will have long since been established and make the traveling of the news perfectly probable.

CHAPTERS 60-61

Summary

A Middlemarch family is moving, and Borthrop Trumbull serves as auctioneer of their belongings. Will, who still lingers in Middlemarch for the purpose of seeing Dorothea once more, goes to the auction to buy a painting for Mrs. Bulstrode at the banker's request. After much buying, noise, and humorous comment, the painting comes up, and Will gets it. On his way out he is approached by a rude stranger who turns out to be John Raffles. Raffles asks if Will's mother's name was Sarah Dunkirk. Will, both annoyed and astonished, answers yes, and after confirming another question about his father's death, gets away. Later the same evening he meets Raffles once more, and this time Raffles is more persistent. He indicates that he knows why Will's mother left her parents — her father had a dishonest business. Will, who only knew that his mother had left home, reflects on what it might mean for his future relationship with Dorothea, if her relatives should hear that Will comes from a dishonorable family.

Raffles goes to see Bulstrode, but finds only the banker's wife at home and goes to the bank. A puzzled Mrs. Bulstrode becomes seriously worried when her husband returns in the evening upset and absentminded. While she tries to find out if the annoying stranger in any way has bothered her husband, Bulstrode's thoughts go back to a past which his wife knows nothing about.

As a young man, Bulstrode had come to know Mr. and Mrs. Dunkirk, a wealthy London couple. Bulstrode was soon taken in as a confidential clerk in Dunkirk's pawnbroking business and learned fast not to ask questions about where some of the merchandise came from. Sarah, the only child after a son had died, ran away from her parents, disapproving of the dishonesty of her father's business, and shortly afterward Mr. Dunkirk died. The

wealthy old widow had come to depend heavily on Mr. Bulstrode's support. Knowing this, Bulstrode suggested marriage,
although many years the younger. She gave her consent after
Bulstrode convinced her that a search after her daughter had
brought no results. Actually the daughter was found, but Raffles,
the only man who knew this besides Bulstrode, was paid to keep
silent. After five years the widow died and left more than 100,000
pounds to a husband she had always thought religious and considerate.

Bulstrode's main worry now is that this ugly story will be
known, and he sends Raffles away with another bribe. He then
offers Will 500 pounds a year, more as an attempt to quiet his
own conscience than as an offer of restitution to Will. Will, who
puts two and two together, refuses to accept any money which
might ruin his honor as a gentleman and angrily leaves the
banker.

Commentary

The lively description of the auction breaks the narrative
for a while, and offers a wealth of humor and local color which
belong to the total picture of Middlemarch. It also serves as an
excellent place for the meeting between Will and Raffles – an
auction at that time being sort of a public entertainment. Thus
it has its place in the development of the plot as well.

Without disturbing the natural sequence of the novel,
George Eliot manages to give us a detailed account of Bulstrode's past. Raffles' presence forces the banker to face a past
he has tried to keep secret, and the reader joins Bulstrode as he
thinks back, still aware of the present time, through the worried
Mrs. Bulstrode.

To alleviate any possible misunderstanding about Bulstrode's hypocritical nature, the author comments directly in
her own character. These asides might seem superfluous, but
they are part of the didactic nature of the novel. The author wants
to be sure that the reader perceives how wrong she considers

Bulstrode's life and actions. He is not only a fictional character; he is a general type of human being that George Eliot wants to expose.

CHAPTER 62

Summary

After two months of indecision Will finally resolves to leave Middlemarch and dispatches a note to Dorothea, requesting a final interview. Dorothea, in the meantime, has gone to Freshitt Hall. Sir James, who has heard rumors about Will and Rosamond, wants to use this to slander Will in Dorothea's eyes. He asks Mrs. Cadwallader to convey the gossip for him. She is more than happy to do her "duty" and informs Dorothea that Will's visits to Rosamond are too frequent to be just polite, social visits. Dorothea angrily lets everyone understand that she refuses to believe this of Will, but she has a disturbing recollection of Rosamond and Will together when she came to see Lydgate on account of Casoubon.

When she goes to Tipton Grange to attend to some matters for her uncle, she finds a surprised Will in the library. The sudden confrontation makes both feel awkward and they are unable to express what they feel. Will tells her he has just heard of the codicil and he regards it as an unjust implication. Dorothea agrees, but also suspects that this is Will's indirect way of telling her he does not love her, and when he tries to tell her in subtle terms about his feelings for her, she thinks he might be referring to Rosamond. Because she is uncertain of Will's feelings, Dorothea also feels she must keep hers secret. Will's departing words, however, give her the assurance she wants, and although he is gone, she is full of joy, thinking he renounces her for honor's sake. Will, on the other hand, must leave for London without any assurance of Dorothea's love.

Commentary

Pride, suspicions, misunderstandings, outside interference, money, honor, timidity, social class are all factors which influence the love story of Will and Dorothea. These elements are perhaps not unique in themselves, but they clarify some of the massiveness of George Eliot's writing. Each factor can actually be traced to a definite source, which has been established earlier in the novel, and by bringing all together in a sort of summary of Will's and Dorothea's love story at this point, the author exemplifies her total control over characters and incidents. She needs to clarify the relationship for transitional purposes yet still keep the reader in suspense about the outcome of the love story. This enables her to return to other characters and conflicts without doing damage to the Dorothea-Will plot.

BOOK SEVEN

CHAPTER 63

Summary

Mr. Farebrother hears about Lydgate's financial problems from the other doctors in Middlemarch. He knows that Lydgate is sensitive about his personal troubles, but resolves to speak to the doctor to see if he can offer any help.

On New Year's Day the Vincy's give a dinner party to honor Mr. Farebrother's new appointment at Lowick. Mary Garth, whom Mrs. Vincy was forced to invite on account of Mary's friendship with the Farebrothers, amuses the children with storytelling, while an always correct Rosamond makes polite excuses for her husband, who has gone to see a patient. Mrs. Farebrother watches the unaffected Mary and silently hopes she will marry her son; Mrs. Vincy sees a plain, insignificant girl whom she does not want in her family. Fred anxiously watches Mary and Mrs. Farebrother to see if he has any reasons for jealousy, and the vicar amuses himself by observing all the contrasts and silent tensions around him.

Lydgate returns, and Farebrother speaks to him in private. He thanks the doctor for mentioning his name to Dorothea and indicates that he would like to be of service in return. Lydgate brushes him off rather impolitely without confiding any of his difficulties.

Commentary

Lydgate's attitude toward Farebrother is a result of his pride. He realizes that the vicar only wishes him well, but he cannot bear the humiliation of admitting that he has failed. In many ways the two men are similar, but Lydgate has not learned to resign himself to misfortune or to accept help when it is offered him.

Notice how the short glimpses of the various characters at the party serve to remind the reader of the traits possessed by each.

CHAPTERS 64-65

Summary

Lydgate's financial problems have become so serious that he asks Mr. Trumbull to find a buyer for the house and the furniture. Rosamond, sensing only the humiliation of losing her home, tells Trumbull to disregard Lydgate's request. Still without her husband's knowledge, she writes a letter to Sir Godwin, Lydgate's rich uncle, asking for financial support.

The morning before her parents' New Year's dinner she informs Lydgate about her transactions with Trumbull. Lydgate, more shocked by her secrecy than angry about her actions, feels helplessly frustrated because he seems unable to communicate with Rosamond. He cannot penetrate her shell of selfishness and her firm belief that the situation is not as serious as he says.

About three weeks after New Year's an answer from Sir Godwin finally arrives. The letter is addressed to Lydgate, and a confident Rosamond waits for him to come home. Lydgate, who at this point has swallowed some of his pride and resolved to go and see his uncle, is surprised to find the letter and furious when he learns its content, realizing that once more his wife has meddled with his affairs.

The letter flatly refuses Rosamond's plea and points out that Lydgate should be man enough to take care of his own business without hiding behind his wife. Lydgate understands that if he tells Rosamond exactly what he thinks, it will ruin his marriage. He therefore calmly asks her only to admit that she has done wrong and to promise that she will never do things in secret again. Rosamond, indignant on her own behalf, keeps silent and regards her husband's language as abusive and insulting. They finally have a reconciliation, Lydgate hoping he will never hate his wife, and Rosamond explaining that she cannot face the humiliation of poverty.

Commentary

Lydgate's bitterness increases when he realizes that his wife will never be able to handle domestic affairs or appreciate his work. He married her for love and he is afraid of losing his affection for her—the only thing which can still make his life bearable. Rosamond, on the other hand, refuses to face any reality which might be unpleasant for herself and also refuses to understand Lydgate's difficulties. Seen in contrast to Lydgate's sincere ambitions, her concerns seem so much the more superficial.

Some of Rosamond's conversation foreshadows later incidents. She wants Lydgate to give up what she feels is his morbid interest in illnesses and rather work to gain more of the profitable kind of patients. She cares nothing about his professional integrity as long as his practice brings money.

Stylistically Sir Godwin's letter is a remnant of an old literary form—the epistolary novel wherein the whole action was conveyed through letters (e.g., Samuel Richardson's *Pamela*). Here the letter serves two purposes which could not have been accomplished by Lydgate's explaining its content: it gives a good characterization of Sir Godwin, a person we never meet; the reader is better able to perceive Lydgate's reaction and how mortifying every word must be to him.

CHAPTER 66

Summary

Although he tries both opium and alcohol, Lydgate's character is too upright for him to become addicted to either, and neither does he have the potential for becoming a gambler. But on one occasion the idea of gambling tempts him. He goes to the Green Dragon to see Bambridge about exchanging his horse for one of lesser quality, and while waiting for the horse-dealer, he starts playing billiards. At first it is only a diversion, but he suddenly realizes how it might bring money and in a sort of trance he starts betting on his own play. Fred Vincy, who has been in the same situation many times himself, walks in, perceives his brother-in-law's intentions and tries to think of a way to get Lydgate away without insulting him. A message from Farebrother, who is waiting downstairs, gives Fred his opportunity. He pulls a dazed Lydgate away from the table, asking him to join him and Farebrother. The doctor suddenly realizes what risks he has been running and abruptly takes his leave.

Farebrother has come to speak to Fred, who, after several months of hard work for Caleb, has once more started to frequent his old spots of entertainment. The vicar explains that he has been tempted to let Fred alone and maybe watch how he would gradually lose Caleb's respect and Mary's love and thus give Farebrother the opportunity to gain her affection. But the vicar is a more righteous man and unselfish friend than that and instead warns Fred to watch his behavior and thereby secure Mary's happiness. Fred sees the danger he has been in and, grateful to Farebrother, he resolves to mend his ways.

Commentary

Different as Lydgate, Fred, and Farebrother are, the way love influences their lives gives them all something in common.

Lydgate's fear of losing his affection for Rosamond because of his money problems makes him for a while as irresponsible as the old Fred; Fred, watching Lydgate's play, comprehends for the first time how gambling can ruin a man, and his reflections are substantiated by Farebrother's advice. Fred's realization brings him closer to Lydgate's belief that personal integrity is necessary for happiness; Farebrother understands how much Mary loves Fred and to secure her happiness he warns Fred — an unselfish act which shows his likeness to Lydgate, who thinks of Rosamond before he thinks of himself.

CHAPTER 67

Summary

Lydgate knows that his only chance is to ask Bulstrode for a loan. He has previously vouched that he will be associated with the banker only through the hospital and is reluctant to make himself dependent on a man he so thoroughly dislikes.

Before Lydgate has made up his mind, Bulstrode informs him that he will be withdrawing his support from the hospital and proposes that Lydgate should contact Mrs. Casoubon for any further aid to the hospital. In spite of this unpleasant news, Lydgate asks Bulstrode for a loan, but the banker only advises him to declare himself bankrupt.

Commentary

Everything Lydgate has planned and worked for crumbles, largely because he is a victim of the hopes, aspirations, and mistakes of other people. Rosamond's selfishness, Bulstrode's fear, and Middlemarch prejudices set up impassable barriers, and Lydgate finds his life directed for him by incidents and emotions which he has no share in himself. This happens to a certain extent in everyone's life, but George Eliot makes Lydgate's life almost totally a result of forces which he cannot control — a tragedy in Lydgate's case because he must have personal freedom in order to develop and extend his medical theories and knowledge.

Summary

Bulstrode's main reason for giving up his support for the hospital is another visit from Raffles. He once more manages to get rid of his now deranged blackmailer, but he is afraid his past will become known and makes plans to leave Middlemarch for an indefinite time. He arranges for Caleb Garth to manage his estate. Caleb, in order to help Mary and Fred, suggests that Fred, under Caleb's supervision, be given the tenancy of Stone Court, and Bulstrode gives his consent.

The same day Bulstrode refuses to help Lydgate, Caleb brings an ill and talkative Raffles to Stone Court. He then goes to the banker, tells him about Raffles and explains that he can no longer remain manager of the estate. Bulstrode immediately understands that Raffles must have told Caleb something and by indicating that Raffles is a liar, he tries to find out how much Caleb knows. The honest man only insists that what he knows will never be repeated and that his conscience forbids him to work for Bulstrode.

Bulstrode calls Lydgate to Stone Court to attend Raffles. When Bulstrode wants to remain with Raffles, Lydgate gives strict regulations about the treatment of the sick man and says that Raffles has a good chance of recovering—something Bulstrode secretly hopes will not happen.

Arriving home, Lydgate finds Rosamond crying and his house in possession of the creditors. For the first time he breaks down in tears and asks Rosamond to share his misfortune with him instead of being against him. The next morning Rosamond speaks of going home to her parents to wait for Lydgate to improve their financial situation. Deeply hurt, Lydgate ironically suggests that he should break his neck, and his life insurance would solve all their problems—a comment which Rosamond takes as an unpleasant, personal insult.

82

Commentary

The stories of Bulstrode and Lydgate are brought closer and closer together. Each is approaching his personal crisis, but the merging of the two stories suggests that eventually they will become involved in a mutual difficulty. In both cases unpredictable circumstances bring about the problems. Since Lydgate is as admirable as Bulstrode is worthy of contempt, it shows how impartial fate can be.

CHAPTER 70

Summary

Lydgate goes to see a slowly recovering Raffles. He gives explicit directions about the amount of opium to be administered to the patient and when it should terminate, and repeats that under no circumstances must he be given liquor. Bulstrode, who is afraid that Lydgate will draw certain conclusions from Raffles' delirious ramblings, lends the doctor 1,000 pounds, thereby hoping to secure his silence. Lydgate is extremely glad to receive the money, and even though it passes through his mind that Bulstrode might have a double motive for this sudden change, he is too happy to worry.

That night Bulstrode lets his housekeeper watch over Raffles while he himself broods over the apparent recovery of the patient. It suddenly dawns on him that he has forgotten to let Mrs. Abel know when to stop the opium dose. He forces himself to go to the room but does not enter. A while later Mrs. Abel asks for some brandy to give Raffles, and after a short fight with himself, Bulstrode gives her the key to the wine cooler, convincing himself that Lydgate's treatment might be wrong and the old remedy of brandy right.

Shortly after Lydgate's arrival the next morning, Raffles dies. The doctor is puzzled, but afraid to insult Bulstrode by asking if his instructions were followed.

Farebrother, who has heard about the procedures at Lydgate's house, comes in the evening to offer his sympathy. Lydgate tells him about the sudden loan. Farebrother is happy on Lydgate's account and listens to Lydgate's enthusiastic plans for the future, plans he can accomplish now that the "torture-screw" is off.

Commentary

Bulstrode's cowardly nature comes clearly to light by his indirect murder of Raffles. When he himself watches Raffles, he cannot change Lydgate's orders. He lets someone else function in his stead and thus feels less guilty.

There is a sad irony in this chapter. Just as Lydgate thinks he is on his way out of his difficulties, the banker gets him involved in more serious problems. At this point the irony is apparent only to the reader—a circumstance which enables the author to keep us in suspense about what will happen to Lydgate. The question of whether Bulstrode's crime will ever be discovered further increases the suspense. Notice how George Eliot puts the reader in a difficult situation at this point. For the sake of what might happen to Lydgate, we would rather have the crime concealed; to punish Bulstrode we would like it to be discovered.

CHAPTER 71

Summary

Bulstrode's feeling of safety turns out to be premature. On a trip north Raffles once related Bulstrode's story to Bambridge, the horse-dealer. A few days after Raffles' death, Bambridge sees Bulstrode, is reminded of the story and tells it to a group of eager listeners. Soon the town buzzes with the gossip and it does not take long before Lydgate's name is connected with the sudden death of Raffles. Everyone knows that Lydgate has borrowed money from the banker, and the idea of a bribe for good service seems extremely likely.

A public meeting is held to determine some new sanitary measures for the town. Bulstrode and Lydgate, neither having yet heard of the gossip, accidentally meet outside and go into the meeting together. Bulstrode, an ardent debater, immediately wants the floor, but is cut short by Mr. Hawley, a lawyer, who requires that Bulstrode first refute Raffles' story. The shock is almost too severe for Bulstrode, but he stands up and accuses Hawley of libel and chicanery. He has no real arguments, however, and the chairman requests that he leave until he can clear himself.

Bulstrode sinks back, and Lydgate, realizing the state of shock he must be in, helps him out, all the while knowing that this must add to the town's suspicions about himself. In a flash he sees how everyone must regard him as the banker's accomplice, and bitter and miserable, the doctor helps the man who has ruined both his life and career.

Farebrother and Brooke go to Lowick and inform Dorothea about the news. After she has asked them to repeat the story, she refuses to believe the accusations against Lydgate and declares that she will work to have his name cleared.

Commentary

Finally the two stories of Bulstrode and Lydgate have conjoined. It has been prepared for all along, and to perceive fully George Eliot's planning for this moment, it is profitable to take a quick, retrospective look at the different episodes which have been utilized for this purpose.

Dorothea, who has not entered the story for some time, is now brought back — and she is brought back partly to advance the development of the Lydgate-Bulstrode plot.

The discovery of Bulstrode's past is coincidental, but even the coincident is made probable. Much earlier in the novel, in connection with Fred, we learn that Bambridge travels around to horse fairs, and he is the right man to go to places which Raffles would frequent. As a horse-dealer, Bambridge is apt to pick up many stories and amusing episodes, and he therefore has no difficulty getting an audience for his story about Bulstrode.

The hasty conclusions about Lydgate are partly due to the earlier antagonism toward him. The major portion of Middlemarch society has been looking for this opportunity to punish Lydgate for his attitude toward them; they welcome the chance to condemn him.

BOOK EIGHT

CHAPTERS 72-75

Summary

Dorothea immediately wants to let Lydgate know of her trust in him, but friends and relatives try to discourage her. At Freshitt Hall Sir James says that Lydgate must clear himself; Mr. Farebrother intimates that Lydgate might actually have been desperate enough to serve Bulstrode; Celia is impatient with her sister because she does not accept Sir James's authority as easily as she accepted Casoubon's; Dorothea is frustrated by their self-protective caution and decides to summon Lydgate, to speak to him about her plans for the hospital and simultaneously to find out the truth behind the slander.

Lydgate first takes Bulstrode home and explains to Mrs. Bulstrode that her husband has had a fainting spell, then rides to town to clear his mind and get rid of his anger. He fully understands the town's suspicions but knows, also, that he cannot accuse Bulstrode of tampering with his instructions regarding the treatment of Raffles, as he has no proof of this. Downcast and lonely, Lydgate can see no way of clearing his name—and even if he could, he would always live with the taint of dishonor. Nevertheless he decides to stay in Middlemarch and by this means at least demonstrates that he has no consciousness of guilt. Returning home, he cannot tell Rosemond anything, fearing what damage this might do to their marriage.

Mrs. Bulstrode, who has been told nothing, realizes from her husband's illness and Lydgate's evasiveness about its cause, that something is being kept from her. She resolves to find out from her friends in Middlemarch what might be the matter, but neither Mrs. Hackbutt nor Mrs. Plymdale give her any exact information; they only show through their unnatural behavior that they know more than she. Fearing the worst, Mrs. Bulstrode goes to her brother, Mr. Vincy, who tells her all. Mrs. Bulstrode, who has always loved her husband and believed him to be morally upright, is crushed. Arriving home she goes to her room, takes off her bright clothes, and puts on a black dress as if she were in mourning, all the while thinking that she has too much affection for her husband ever to leave him. In the evening she finally goes to see Bulstrode, who immediately comprehends that she knows all, and they cry together, in mutual sympathy and distress.

Bulstrode's money solved one of the main obstacles to Rosamond's happiness with Lydgate. Still, she is bored because Will's departure for London has robbed her of the continued admiration of a young, agreeable man. Lydgate, who cannot make himself speak to Rosamond about all his difficulties, goes around with a troubled mind and only increases Rosamond's ennui. The doctor receives a letter from Will, who announces his return to Middlemarch. This pleases Rosamond, who consequently plans a dinner party to celebrate the coming of happier times. She sends out invitations, as usual without her husband's knowledge, but they are all politely refused.

Rosamond goes to her parents' house and finally hears the story. She can see what this might mean for herself in the form of humiliating talk in the town and determines to make Lydgate leave Middlemarch for London, but she mentions nothing to her husband.

Lydgate feels her silent repugnance and antagonism and asks if she knows, expressing hope that she realizes his innocence. Rosamond makes no concession about her beliefs either way and instead pleads for an early departure for London, where no one will know of the disgrace. Lydgate tries to make her understand that he must stay in Middlemarch, but her answer is a hostile silence. Desperate about his wife's refusal to support him, Lydgate leaves the room, while an equally upset Rosamond longs for Will, who can listen to her problems with sympathy.

Commentary

In turn, each of these chapters describes the reactions and thoughts of the people who have become directly involved in the story which has become *the* topic of interest in Middlemarch. Dorothea and Rosamond naturally furnish the most obvious contrast. The former voluntarily chooses a part which will enable her to help a man she believes in; her decision to do this is the more admirable since she is only interested in Lydgate for humane reasons; she cannot stand still and see a man condemned without proof. This should have been the part normally belonging to Lydgate's wife, but Rosamond is incapable of sharing any of her husband's suffering; her nature lacks any deep feeling, and she can see only an immediate escape as a solution.

Mrs. Bulstrode, although not of the sharpest intellect, has an affectionate nature, and even when she knows the worst, her love is stronger than her shame. She has much more to blame her husband for than Rosamond can ever charge against Lydgate, but in a true Christian spirit she practices forgiveness rather than adding more misery.

Lydgate, the man who really suffers for Bulstrode's actions, shows his courage when he decides to remain in Middlemarch. He knows that escape will never free him from suspicion, and he wants to live out a difficult period to regain his honor even if it might never be totally restored.

Bulstrode's reaction proves his weakness. He has no courage to come out and declare Lydgate's innocence, which in turn would mean total disgrace for himself. He takes refuge in his wife's compassion and only wants to go some place where he once more can gradually forget the disgrace of his past.

Rosamond resembles Bulstrode in her desire to run away from the difficulties. Lydgate's courage is echoed in Dorothea, while Dorothea's warm nature is reflected in Mrs. Bulstrode.

The similarities and contrasts presented in these four chapters represent a little world in miniature: What happens to a human being when he has to face an ethical problem and when his behavior of the moment determines what people will think of him the remainder of his life? What happens to people who have to choose whether they want to become involved in another man's difficulty at the risk of their being connected with his disgrace? George Eliot offers a variety of answers, but the tone which accompanies the description of each person, leaves no doubt as to where her sympathies lie.

Notice how the chapters move from the reaction of the peripheral characters at Freshitt Hall to Lydgate, who is the principal character in the conflict—a development which steadily intensifies the suspense.

CHAPTERS 76-77

Summary

Bulstrode once more decides to depart from Middlemarch and leaves it to Dorothea to continue the support of the hospital. She finally gets her opportunity to speak to Lydgate without making him feel that she is interfering in his private life. Tactfully she manages to gain his full confidence. Lydgate, relieved to have found an unsuspicious, sympathetic listener, gives her the facts as he knows them. Dorothea assures him that she has full faith in his innocence and that she will convey her conviction to her relatives and Farebrother and thereby gain more support for the doctor.

She also shows him some of her plans for the hospital and asks him to work with her. Lydgate remembers Rosamond's demand and answers that although grateful to Dorothea, he must leave Middlemarch on account of his wife. Dorothea can appreciate his predicament, having had difficulties in her own marriage, and she makes Lydgate promise not to make any arrangements until she has spoken to Rosamond. Lydgate silently doubts that Dorothea's efforts will make much difference, but her sympathy has restored some of his spirits.

To alleviate one of Lydgate's problems immediately, Dorothea decides to give him 1,000 pounds to relieve him of his obligation to Bulstrode. She writes a check, which she plans to bring with her when she visits Rosamond.

Rosamond has written a letter to Will Ladislaw asking him to hasten his intention of coming. She desires his diverting company and also wants his help in convincing Lydgate to go to London.

Dorothea, busy with plans for Lydgate, knows she cannot approach Rosamond directly about her marriage to the doctor, but she hopes that she will be able to convince Rosamond of the importance of Lydgate's staying in Middlemarch. When Dorothea arrives on her visit, the housekeeper thinks her mistress is upstairs and shows Dorothea into the living room to wait. Dorothea enters and discovers Rosamond and Will, looking intently at each other. Will, holding Rosamond's hands, speaks to her in a soft voice. Rosamond immediately stands up, while Will looks confused and bothered. Dorothea, remembering the gossip about Rosamond and Will, receives a terrible shock, but manages to keep her composure. She delivers the letter with the check and immediately walks out. Reaching the carriage, she can only think of Will courting Rosamond behind Lydgate's back, and to forget this ugly picture, she forces herself to remain extremely busy the rest of the day.

Commentary

Dorothea's compassion for Lydgate and his problems is mainly a result of her general knowledge of human nature. She is aware of Lydgate's capacities and understands how his pride must smart under the unjust accusations against his professional and personal ethics. In addition, her own experiences enable her to perceive Lydgate's marriage problems.

At this point the stories of Dorothea and Lydgate have definitely become expressions of a similar theme. Both are genuinely interested in human improvement, but society and marriage present them with difficulties they never anticipated. In connection with Lydgate's feelings and considerations for Rosamond, it seems appropriate to contemplate how Dorothea's life and attitudes would have been had Casoubon lived.

George Eliot makes the meeting of Dorothea, Rosamond, and Will as effective as possible by carefully introducing the chapter with an account of both women's feelings toward Will, while mentioning nothing of Will's feelings.

Minute details characterize the description of Dorothea's entrance into the living room and furnish another example of the author's consideration for the probability of an episode. Dorothea's discovery of Will and Rosamond must be a complete surprise to all three to make a real impact on the reader, and every step Dorothea takes, and the noiselessness of the door she enters through, makes the reactions of the discoverer, as well as the discovered, perfectly believable.

CHAPTERS 78-79

Summary

A startled Rosamond and Will watch Dorothea's entrance and quick departure, and Will immediately knows what Dorothea must think. Furiously he lashes out at Rosamond. Knowing that he is unjust, he still blames her for having ruined his whole life. Rosamond cowers under his anger and the knowledge that Will has never really been interested in her. After Will has gone, Rosamond lies down on her bed, feeling ill from the upsetting episode. When Lydgate comes home, she breaks into hysterical crying. Lydgate, knowing that Dorothea was supposed to visit, thinks Rosamond's tears indicate that she finally admits how wrongly she has treated him.

After consoling his wife, Lydgate finds Dorothea's letter, which confirms that Dorothea was there in the morning. Will returns to see Lydgate, who knows nothing about what actually happened earlier. Lydgate informs Will that the latter's name is mentioned in connection with the Bulstrode scandal and that most Middlemarchers are against him because he is part Jew. Will takes this fairly lightly, having more serious worries about Dorothea.

Commentary

Will's reaction, which is hardly justified, proves how strongly he loves Dorothea. Strong emotions usually promise irrational behavior, and when Dorothea leaves, Will can picture her walking out of his life forever. But compared to Dorothea's determination to control her feelings, his anger seems to indicate a certain amount of immaturity.

Will's fury teaches Rosamond two things: a man's attention is not always a result of everlasting admiration and love—a crushing experience for Rosamond, who has always taken men's admiration for granted; she learns that she cannot automatically control a man's anger at herself—a discovery which momentarily makes her more compassionate toward her husband, who always ends by asking her forgiveness.

The reaction against Will is increased by his being part Jew and is an additional comment on how prejudices can lead to difficulties. Although she only touches upon the problem in this novel, George Eliot was an ardent spokesman against antisemitism. Her last novel, *Daniel Deronda*, treats the problem extensively.

CHAPTERS 80-81

Summary

Dorothea manages to keep going all day, and she finally reaches the Farebrothers, where she stays for dinner. Henrietta

Noble, Farebrother's old aunt, complains about having lost a candy box which was given her by her beloved Will Ladislaw. At the mention of his name all Dorothea's emotions come rushing back.

Alone in her room she finally admits to herself what the loss of Will means. Sobbing from the anguish of his betrayal, she falls asleep on the hard, cold floor. She wakes next morning in a calmer mood, and her feelings of self-pity are gone. She resigns herself to the inevitable and starts once more to think of her duties. With the resolve that she has no right to be bitter, she once more goes to Middlemarch to "save Rosamond" and the doctor's marriage.

When·Rosamond hears of Dorothea's arrival, she becomes both confused and frightened, but Dorothea's gentle courtesy assures her that she has nothing to fear. While Dorothea speaks about Lydgate and why he should stay in Middlemarch, Rosamond thinks of the kindness of the woman she thought would be filled with hate, and, ashamed, she bursts into tears. Dorothea goes on to speak of mutual love and fidelity as necessary for a happy marriage, and Rosamond suddenly understands the agony Dorothea must feel after seeing Will and herself. Influenced by Dorothea's compassion, she explains what actually happened. Will had been telling her of his strong love for Dorothea so that Rosamond might know he could never love her. This almost benumbs Dorothea, who can only sense that it will "be joy when she ha[s] recovered her power of feeling it," and after a few more remarks to Rosamond about Lydgate, she leaves.

Commentary

Even when she has Rosamond's assurance that Will loves her, Dorothea tries to control her emotions. This is a character trait which is part of her independent nature. She does not like other people to know her innermost thoughts; experience has taught her that emotional expressions can be misunderstood. Because she cannot openly express her feelings, she often finds herself in an isolated, lonely position. When she discovered that she had no love left for Casoubon, her respect for the marriage vows prevented her indicating any of her problems to anyone; before Will leaves for London she hesitates to say anything about her affection for him, since she is not sure of his love for her. She is constantly surrounded by people who let their feelings rule their rational faculties, but out of self-protection and consideration for other people, Dorothea cannot give herself away that easily.

By telling Dorothea the truth about Will and herself, Rosamond for once acts unselfishly. It is not a lasting change in her nature — she is too shallow actually to learn anything from her short contact with Dorothea. It is still a tiny example of what Rosamond could have been had she not been spoiled and pampered all her life. Her reaction is also an additional comment on Dorothea's effect on other people.

CHAPTERS 82-84

Summary

Will's disappointment almost drives him away from Middlemarch again, but he goes back to apologize for his unjust behavior to Rosamond. Rosamond treats him coldly, but lets him know that she has explained the circumstances to Dorothea. Not knowing whether the incident has damaged his relations with Dorothea forever, Will goes once more to say good-bye to her. They almost repeat the mistake of their last farewell, but just as Will is leaving, Dorothea disregards pride, controlled emotions, and timidity, and exclaims: "Oh, I cannot bear it — my heart will break."

Mr. Brooke brings the news to Freshitt Hall that Dorothea and Will plan to marry in three weeks. Everyone is astonished, including the visiting Cadwalladers, and Sir James swears he will never see Dorothea again. Celia goes to Lowick to make her sister change her mind and save the family from what everyone feels will be total disgrace. For the last time, however, Dorothea proves that she is strongly independent and only tells her sister how happy she knows she will be with Will.

Commentary

Several critics feel that Will is not worthy of Dorothea, and that George Eliot made a mistake in letting a woman with Dorothea's fine mind marry the less credibly realized Will. One must agree that compared to the strong masculinity of the seriously dedicated Lydgate, Will seems less of a hero. On the other hand, Will has a strong sense of honor, and he finally ends up as a successful man. It is also necessary to grant that George Eliot was not trying to create a happy fairy tale where the best man gets the best girl. She presents a picture of life which is real rather than ideal.

CHAPTERS 85-86

Summary

Mr. Bulstrode, who has sent his daughters away to school, prepares to leave Middlemarch. He has become mainly concerned about his wife, whose suffering has been immense, and he asks her if there is anything she wants to settle before they leave. She suggests that they try to give some help to Rosamond, but since Lydgate has returned the check, Bulstrode believes the doctor will refuse any aid. In order to do something for her family, Mrs. Bulstrode then arranges with Caleb to put Fred in charge of Stone Court.

Caleb, careful as always, finds out for certain that Mary's love for Fred is genuine and then lets a happy, young couple know that Fred's prospects for the future seem good. Mary can marry the manager of an estate instead of the caricature of a minister.

Commentary

The rounding up of the Bulstrode plot is short and effective. He has already lost our interest as a character because we know every fault he has, and all that is necessary to know is that he will never again be able to escape his past; he needs only to look at his wife to see how he has changed her from a healthy, happy woman to a reflective, sick, though always affectionate, companion.

The completion of Fred and Mary's love story is equally short, but once more George Eliot demonstrates her genius for plot structure. She connects the happiness of Fred and Mary with the unhappiness of the Bulstrodes. Because Bulstrode must leave, Fred becomes his manager, and the author has accomplished a final tying together of original separate stories.

FINALE

Summary

"Who can quit young lives after being long in company with them, and not desire to know what befell them in their after-years?"

Although Fred never became rich, he and Mary were happy in their marriage and were blessed with three sons. Lydgate became a successful physician for a high society clientele, alternating between London and a Continental resort. He could never forget that he was forced to give up his medical research and, an embittered man, he died at fifty, leaving Rosamond and four daughters behind. Rosamond married an elderly and wealthy physician shortly afterward.

Dorothea never regretted that she gave up position and fortune to marry Will. Their marriage was full of love, and they had two children. Will eventually became a member of Parliament and worked diligently for various reforms. The birth of their first son brought about a reconciliation with Celia and Sir James, and the Ladislaws started leaving London twice a year to visit with the Chettams and their several children at Freshitt Hall. Mr. Brooke, who lived to be an old man, left his estate to Dorothea's son.

The Middlemarchers always regarded Dorothea's marriage as a mistake and felt she had married a man whom they could never accept.

Commentary

The final summing up of the novel's many plots and characters is in tradition with nineteenth-century writing. Everything had to be concluded in such a way that the reader would never wonder about the fates of any of the principal characters. These last comments might seem superfluous to the modern reader. On the other hand, they fit the total structure of the novel. Just as the separate incidents are given a beginning and an end, the lives of the characters are not completed until we know how their lives turn out after all the various and dramatic episodes they have been through.

It is worthwhile to compare the Dorothea of the first chapters to the Dorothea who has become Will's wife. She changes from an idealistic girl to a wise woman. She keeps her warm interest in human beings and their welfare, but she resigns herself to becoming a good wife for the man she loves, rather than "performing heroic deeds." She does not become a modern St. Theresa, but one of the many admirable people who influence the "growing good of the world" and who prove "that things are not so ill with you and me as they might have been."

Analysis of Main Characters

ARTHUR BROOKE

Brooke is a man with limited views and ideas, who likes to think of himself as a liberal and progressive reformer. He is always willing to voice his opinion, and often on subjects he knows nothing about. Believing in his own good intentions, he tries to give advice to everyone, but a little criticism can easily make him change his mind. He wants to be appreciated and he dislikes spending his money. The last two characteristics ultimately direct most of his actions.

DOROTHEA BROOKE
(MRS. CASOUBON; MRS. LADISLAW)

Dorothea is an attractive young woman whose ideals and ideas set her apart from the standard nineteenth-century conceptions of a woman. She desires "masculine knowledge" and has hopes of accomplishing great tasks. She is an emancipated St. Theresa whose compassion for mankind makes her an ardent spokeswoman for social reform and justice.

Dorothea's independence expresses itself in various ways. Contrary to her relatives' desire, she marries the much-older Casoubon in an effort to obtain scholastic learning and an opportunity to serve mankind. Her decision is defiant because a woman in the mid-nineteenth century was expected to comply with her family's wishes, and because marriage was largely a matter of choosing the best economic supporter. On her own Dorothea makes plans and designs which will improve the living conditions of her uncle's tenants, and she defies anyone who wants her to remain at home with embroidery and innocent poetry books.

Total honesty toward herself and others characterizes much of Dorothea's behavior. She takes the full consequences of her actions and dislikes anyone who compromises with the truth in order to escape momentary or permanent difficulties. She has a strong sense of duty and, although it sometimes gives her personal problems, she always remains loyal to her promises.

Dorothea displays strength and courage when she defies a whole town in her support of the unjustly disgraced Doctor Lydgate. She believes in knowing the circumstances before making a judgment, and she never lets personal prejudice influence her benevolence toward other people. Her interest in people is sincere and directed toward social as well as legal justice.

She possesses feelings and passions which belong to any normal, young girl, but she also has the self-control to curb any excessive expression of emotion. When she wakes up to real love, she accepts the fact that love means sharing, and she can freely give up some of her plans to make a happy life for herself as well as for Will Ladislaw, her second husband.

Finally, Dorothea is a proud woman, but never unjustly so. Her pride comes from a firm belief in her own moral and intellectual integrity, and because her actions are motivated by just, although sometimes loftily remote, considerations, she is a woman to be admired.

CELIA BROOKE (LADY CHETTAM)

Although younger than Dorothea, Celia has a greater capacity for seeing reality than her sister. She is far less intense and her aspirations are those of a normal, well brought up young lady. She is totally satisfied with an appropriate marriage and she likes to fulfill the standard functions required of her as mother and wife. Her sense of humor shows that she has a good eye for the ridiculous, and her concern for her sister's welfare shows her genuinely affectionate heart.

EDWARD CASOUBON

Dorothea's first husband is in many ways a pitiable character. His whole life is one desperate attempt to achieve a goal he knows is too ambitious. The fear of humiliation makes him continue working on a book which would be insignificant even if it were to be finished. His intellect is mediocre and his scholarly pride wholly unrealistic.

Emotionally selfish, Casoubon has no capacity for large feelings and considerations, and his love for Dorothea is mainly the desire to gain a companion for his aging years. Suspecting an affair between Dorothea and his cousin Will Ladislaw, he demonstrates how fully vanity and jealousy govern his imagination. His constant frustrations have made him a suspicious man and he sees schemes against himself where there are none.

In spite of these unlikable traits, Casoubon is also tragic. He suffers genuinely from his own inabilities and his life, which he knows is consumed in a waste of time and energy, becomes pitiable because he is aware of his limitations but too proud to admit them.

SIR JAMES CHETTAM

As a young baronet Sir James is much concerned about social propriety. Although benevolent and seriously interested in social reforms, he will let nothing interfere with his conviction that social distinctions should be maintained and that the English gentleman is of a superior kind. He likes to think that his opinions are correct and his prejudices justified; when they are disputed, he tends to feel insulted. Being a good-looking man, he is somewhat vain. He is generally amiable and becomes a good husband and father.

WILL LADISLAW

Dorothea's second husband at first seems to be a somewhat irresponsible, flippant man. He is artistically inclined, but changes from one art form to the other without any serious ambitions. He is an honorable gentleman and an eloquent conversationalist—with a good deal of humor.

He has a careless attitude toward people in general and no desires to deepen or extend the superficial acquaintances he makes. His love for Dorothea makes him a man of more substantial quality. His leisurely interest in politics grows sincere and he eventually becomes a respected politician.

Although his mind and his capacity for human compassion are more shallow than Dorothea's, his sense of honesty is just as strong. He abhors hypocrisy and would never do anything which would damage his honor as a gentleman and moral man.

TERTIUS LYDGATE

The young Dr. Lydgate is in many ways Dorothea's male counterpart. He is bright and ambitious and wants to devote his time to scientific research, which eventually will be of benefit to mankind. He would rather bring true relief to the poor than prescribe worthless medicine to wealthy hypochondriacs.

He is morally sound and his scorn for dishonesty is as severe as Will's. When the other doctors turn against him because he is a stranger and because he uses newer methods than they, he cannot compromise. He knows his medical knowledge is superior and refuses to let their pettiness influence him.

Upright and strong as his personality is, it is marred by a few "spots of commonness." "That distinction of mind which belonged to his intellectual ardour, did not penetrate his feeling and judgment about furniture, or women, or the desirability of its being known that he was better born than other country surgeons." Lydgate is socially arrogant and he pays severely for this. He becomes attracted to Rosamond Vincy, the only girl who seems to possess the social graces he requires of a woman, and he binds himself forever to a wife who has no appreciation for his finer qualities.

That he remains loyal to his wife, even after he no longer really loves her, shows his capacity for compassion as well as responsibility. He admits his own share in the unfortunate marriage, and he takes the consequences of his decisions. His wife's impossible actions make his temper flare, but he compromises because the tender part of his nature is stronger than his egotism.

ROSAMOND VINCY *(MRS. LYDGATE)*

Rosamond is spoiled and selfish, and has none of the intellectual capacities which a man of Lydgate's caliber needs. She is incapable of understanding that her decisions are sometimes wrong—even ruinous. When something goes against her own perception of what is necessary, she has a stubborn capacity for refusing to understand that someone else might be right.

Her vanity is obvious. She is a social climber and wants to be admired by everyone. Any criticism or indication of dislike, however just it might be, she regards as an insult. She is incapable of realistic judgment, and she can lie both to others and to herself without any feeling of remorse. Even her love is motivated by her selfishness. She marries Lydgate for the money and the social position he might give her, and as long as he seems to maintain these, she is satisfied. Whenever her husband asks for any support which might mean unpleasant exertion, she simply refuses, feeling absolutely justified in doing so.

FRED VINCY

Fred is a spoiled young man whose sense of responsibility grows through his contact with Mary Garth and her family. He is good-natured and willing to prove himself once he is assured of Mary's love. In contrast to the rest of his family, he is almost free of social snobbery, and he has enough courage to defy their opinions in order to marry for love.

MARY GARTH

Mary, although plain, is an admirable girl. She has a sense of honesty which permits no one or nothing to interfere with her beliefs of what is right and wrong. She has a good eye for the humorous in a situation; she mainly laughs at the folly and prejudices of the selfish people that surround her, but she is not afraid to see herself in a sarcastic light. Bright and with a natural curiosity, she likes to read. She has a warm nature which makes her a good companion for those who know how to appreciate sincere feelings.

NICHOLAS BULSTRODE

The banker in Middlemarch is first and foremost a hypocrite. He wants to be respected as a pious man and constantly exaggerates his own morality and piety.

The real Bulstrode is a sad case of dishonesty, cowardice, and even criminal actions. He has a marvelous ability to excuse his own wrongs, and by a small atonement he always pacifies an easily subdued conscience.

Critical Analysis

THE UNITY OF PLOTS AND THEMES

The novel's subtitle, *Life in a Provincial Town,* indicates that George Eliot wanted her book to represent a picture of an isolated, small, but nevertheless completed world. It might seem presumptuous to call her portrait of Middlemarch and its inhabitants a mirror of society as the author perceived it, but the conflicts, frustrations, relationships, and problems belonging to the Middlemarchers are connected with very basic elements of life, such as love, money and ambition, religion and ethics.

The four main actions which constitute the full plot of the novel, all emphasize one or more of these aspects. The Dorothea-Casoubon relationship shows how two people with very different ideas on love and existence can find something in each other because they mistake egocentric motives for indications of love. When both realize that their feelings are not reciprocal, the love disappears, and the husband and wife become two miserable people who cannot escape their own mistakes and they suffer for it.

For Lydgate and Rosamond the lack of money and contrary ambitions destroy most of the feeling that first created the marriage. Lydgate is by far the greater sufferer in the relationship, since his whole life's purpose is ruined by the petty ambitions of his wife. Seen as a variation of the situation of Dorothea and Casoubon, the two plots supply, between them, deeply explored examples of how it is possible to ruin one's life by mistaking one's own thoughts and ideas for those of another. For Lydgate his marriage is disastrous; Dorothea escapes such a tragedy only by the timely death of Casoubon.

The third love-relationship in the novel, that of Fred and Mary, is much less profoundly explored, but the triangle situation, which includes Mr. Farebrother, shows how the knots and tangles can be untied if selfless consideration rather than egotism decides. Farebrother's love is selfless, since he recognizes Mary's feelings for Fred and renounces his own claims on her in order to see her happy. The sensibility of Mary demonstrates, in contrast to the other two love stories, that love need not be irrational but can be, when it is the expression of an emotional and moral maturity, a stabilizing force. Seen in juxtaposition with one another, these three major love plots and the final love story of Dorothea and Will indicate the variety and depth of the author's thoughts about the Victorian Adam and Eve.

The Bulstrode plot, concerned mainly with the hypocrisy which desire for wealth and respectability can lead to, is a variation of the author's concern with selfishness. Bulstrode, a man of weak ethical principles, is tempted by the security of money as the other characters are tempted by their ideas of love. His indirect responsibility for Raffles' death and Lydgate's disgrace reveals the extent of the evil to which this kind of desire can lead.

Although the four plots are variously and complexly developed, their successful union as one main action demonstrates George Eliot's superb ability to create a firm structure out of richly diverse materials. The interactions of the multitudinous characters are achieved gradually, and what might at first seem the beginnings of entirely new stories are by the end of the novel so interconnected that no one part could be eliminated without seriously injuring the unity of the whole. Thematic parallels between the different plots are developed and fused into one large conception, and this conception presents life as it specifically occurs in Middlemarch but as it could generally occur anywhere. George Eliot's novels are sometimes criticized for containing too many details and elaborate explanations. We must keep in mind, however, the Victorian fictional tradition of leaving no aspect of a story unexplained or unfinished, and George Eliot shows how it can be done without seeming un-lifelike.

HUMOR

The novel's themes are mainly serious and include philosophical speculations about life and its various problems. The novel never becomes indigestibly heavy, however, for the seriousness is periodically broken by humorous comments, incidents, and characters.

The variety of minor characters contributes much toward the lighter and often sarcastic tone of the novel. People like Mrs. Cadwallader, Mr. Featherstone, Mr. Trumbull, Henrietta Noble—and others—are vividly captured and displayed, and their attitudes and actions display George Eliot's deep knowledge of her own creations and show how she could delineate them with good-humored accuracy. Mrs. Cadwallader's inexhaustible plans for advantageous matchmaking are examples of snobbery, but since they never seriously injure anyone, they become only ludicrous. Featherstone reveals a blacker kind of humor. His passion for money is repellent but his delight in skillfully playing with his relations as a cat plays with a mouse is amusing because it demonstrates so well his relatives' stupidity and greed.

Many of the incidents that show the incredible egotism and pride of the characters also serve to create humor. Naumann's satirical account of Casoubon's image of himself, based on unwarranted self-esteem, is amusing as well as severe. Mr. Brooke's pompously unrealistic faith in his own abilities is cruelly deflated when he addresses the crowd and makes a fool of himself.

Humor untinged with irony or sarcasm can be found in the scenes in which we share Mrs. Garth's daily life. The scene in her kitchen, when she attempts to function as teacher, washerwoman, baker, and mother at one and the same time, is a warm, smiling description of a happy family.

The author's comments, which regularly interrupt the narrative, are frequently colored by sutble humor. This humor can be found in the words and images chosen to enhance the fictional descriptions, or it can often be detected in the lengthier comments on the vanities and stupidities involving so many of the characters.

THE THEME OF DISENCHANTMENT

It has been said by many critics that George Eliot's novels represent "psychological realism" and that this can be seen again and again in her treatment of the theme of illusion versus reality. In *Middlemarch* the conflicts of the characters frequently arise from their tragic inability to judge the world as it truly is. In Dorothea's case the disenchantment consists of a gradual realization of her husband's limitations, and she must learn how to live with the facts; Lydgate must learn to accept the true, selfish personality of his wife and what this will mean to him professionally and personally; Fred Vincy must learn that life consists of more serious tasks than waiting for the inheritance of a rich uncle.

A variant of the theme of disenchantment is represented in Casoubon. Rather than trying to discover the facts, he acts on his jealousy, which is based upon a false conception of the relationship between Dorothea and Will. Pride likewise prevents him from openly admitting his own limitations and he tries to live on an illusion about his own powers, all the while suffering because he has moments of insight which reveal his own insignificance.

Bulstrode tries to suppress reality entirely and creates an illusionary image of himself in which he believes. When the truth comes to light, his punishment is severe because the reality he tries to forget is so hideous. He finally learns that living on illusions and untrue representations is wrong, and the disenchantment makes him a more humble and acceptable person.

Review Questions and Essay Topics

1. Show how George Eliot aids her characterizations by presenting contrasting figures.

2. Trace the dark-light imagery connected with Casoubon, Dorothea, and Will.

3. Choose a passage of particularly detailed description and discuss its form and function.

4. Discuss one or more of George Eliot's means of transition between the different plots.

5. How does George Eliot show her firm belief that women were more than domestic servants?

6. What is the function of the author's direct comments?

7. Discuss the value of giving retrospective accounts of actions and characters.

8. How does George Eliot achieve local color in the novel?

9. How does the interference of the author sometimes create suspense for the reader?

10. What are the reasons for the misunderstandings between Will and Dorothea before their marriage? What are the reasons for the misunderstandings between Lydgate and Rosamond before and after their marriage?

11. Is Caleb Garth's honesty and goodness totally believable?

12. Explain some of the functions of the various minor characters.

13. In what way do the episodes surrounding Peter Featherstone enhance the meaning of the novel?

14. Discuss the novel's use of coincidence and then show how it is incorporated into the more obvious cause-effect developments.

Selected Bibliography

ANDERSON, QUENTIN. "George Eliot in *Middlemarch.*" *From Dickens to Hardy,* ed. BORIS FORD. Baltimore, 1958. An analysis which shows George Eliot's position among other nineteenth-century novelists.

BEATY, JEROME. *Middlemarch from Notebook to Novel: A study of George Eliot's Creative Method.* Urbana, 1960. This study shows in detail the characteristics of the novel's structure.

BENNETT, JOAN. *George Eliot.* Cambridge, 1962. Probably the best introduction to the life and works of George Eliot.

CARROLL, DAVID. "Unity through Analogy: An Interpretation of *Middlemarch.*" *Victorian Studies,* II (1959), 305-16. A brief article which points out the parallels between the developments of various characters and their fates.

HARDY, BARBARA. "The Moment of Disenchantment in George Eliot's Novels." *Review of English Studies,* n.s., V (1954), 256-64. A good, general introduction to this special problem appearing over and over in George Eliot's novels.

JAMES, HENRY. "George Eliot's *Middlemarch.*" *Nineteenth Century Fiction,* VIII (1953), 161-70. An interesting article showing how an almost contemporary novelist viewed George Eliot's writing.

PARIS, BERNARD J. *Experiments in Life.* Detroit, 1965. A solid study of George Eliot's ideas seen in relation to her own time. It shows the author's intellectual development and how the novels exemplify her search for values in a godless universe.

THALE, JEROME. *The Novels of George Eliot.* New York, 1959. A historic analysis of George Eliot's novels showing the author's place in the tradition of English fictional writing.